MARCO  POLO

C000171558

PHUKET

CHINA

MYANMAR   LAOS

Gulf of   South
                              China Sea
Bengal   THAI-
               LAND
               Bangkok
Andaman   CAMBODIA VIET-
Islands   NAM

INDIAN
OCEAN
         Phuket
                    MALAYSIA
         INDONESIA

www.marco-polo.com

The best Insider Tips → p. 4

INSIDER TIP

Best of ... → p. 6

The West Coast → p. 32

South and East Coast → p. 58

SYMBOLS

INSIDER TIP	Insider Tip
★	Highlight
●●●●	Best of ...
⊰⊱	Scenic view
☺	Responsible travel: fair trade principles and the environment respected
(*)	Telephone numbers that are not toll-free

**PRICE CATEGORIES
HOTELS**

Expensive	over 2,660 baht
Moderate	1,520–2,660 baht
Budget	under 1,520 baht

Prices are for two people in a double room or for a bunga-low in a beach resort

**PRICE CATEGORIES
RESTAURANTS**

Expensive	over 380 baht
Moderate	190–380 baht
Budget	under 190 baht

Prices are for a two-course meal without drinks

On the cover: Ko Phi Phi – a dream island and diver's paradise p. 76 | Tranquil Phang Nga Bay p. 74

CONTENTS

Phuket Town → p. 66

Destinations around Phuket → p. 7

Trips & Tours → p. 84

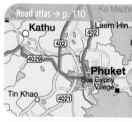
Road atlas → p. 110

MAPS IN THE GUIDEBOOK
(112 A1) Page numbers and coordinates refer to the road atlas
(0) Site/address located off the map.
Coordinates are also given for places that are not marked on the road atlas
(U A1) Coordinates for the map of Phuket Town in the back cover.
Karon, Kata Noi Beach → p. 41
Patong → p. 51

INSIDE BACK COVER: PULL-OUT MAP →

PULL-OUT MAP 𝄞
(𝄞 A–B 2–3) Refers to the removable pull-out map
(𝄞 a–b 2–3) refers to the additional maps on the pull-out map

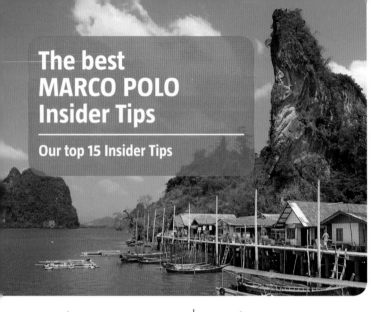

The best MARCO POLO Insider Tips

Our top 15 Insider Tips

INSIDERTIP Yoga on a beach to dream of

Om... – in the exclusive Renaissance resort on Mai Khao Beach you can relax completely during yoga sessions on the island's longest beaches → p. 46

INSIDERTIP A balcony above the sea

Everyone knows Cape Promthep on Phuket. But there is also a lookout spot high above the bay of Nai Harn, where you don't have to share your dream view of the sea with crowds of tourists → p. 64

INSIDERTIP Mother's cooking

Suntisook Resort on Ko Yao Noi has more than cosy bungalows. When the lady of the house serves up mashed potatoes there, you will feel you're back home → p. 82

INSIDERTIP Acquire the taste

Feel the sand under your feet while dining well at Taste on Surin Beach → p. 56

INSIDERTIP Fall in love with this place

The name says it all: Je t'aime on Ko Yao Noi is a pretty café where you can fall in love with this unspoiled island while enjoying your meal, coffee or cocktails → p. 80

INSIDERTIP Fine dining in a historic location

Enjoy top Thai cooking in a beautifully restored town house in the Sino-Portuguese style at the China Inn in Phuket Town (photo right) → p. 69

INSIDERTIP Putting in the dark

Golf beneath floodlights? Why not? On Phunaka Golf Course near Chalong you can practise teeing off at night → p. 92

INSIDERTIP A personal touch

The Heimat Gardens guesthouse on Ko Yao Yai is run by multilingual Yamalia, who likes to show her guests a slice of real Thai life → p. 83

BEST OF ...

FOR FREE

● *A walk through the swamp*

In *Sirinat National Park* you can walk through a swamp while keeping your feet dry. The boardwalks allow you to discover a fascinating eco-system. And there is no admission fee for this part of the national park → p. 45

● *Panorama postcard from the summit*

Get a breathtaking view without feeling shattered: climb the 348 steep steps to the *viewpoint* and watch the twin bays of Ko Phi Phi shimmering beneath you and massive cliffs with green tops rising from the sea ... → p. 76

● *A visit to the Chinese gods*

Many residents of Phuket have Chinese ancestors and still worship the gods of those ancestors. You can pay your respects to them in the col-ourful *Jui Tui Temple* in Phuket Town: from Tean Hu Huan Soy, the god associated with artists, to Kiu Wong (photo) the vegetarian god → p. 66

● *Old Phuket in black and white*

A free trip back in time: in the *Old Phuket Gallery* you can do some shopping, but also see how things looked in Phuket Town before the tourists came. Old photos show views of the town from the days when rickshaw drivers would pedal around here → p. 70

● *Majestic tower*

The *lighthouse on Cape Promthep* was built in honour of the king. Not only does it command a fantastic view of the south coast of Phuket, inside you can admire sextants and marine charts free of charge → p. 64

● *Buried Buddha*

This Enlightened One is definitely worth seeing: the *Golden Buddha in Wat Phra Thong* is firmly planted in the ground – only the upper part of his body is visible. According to a legend, anyone who tries to dig out the statue will die. It costs nothing – and is perfectly safe... - to take a look → p. 37

●●●● Dots in guidebook refer to 'Best of ...' tips

ONLY IN PHUKET
Unique experiences

● *Colonial atmosphere*
Thailand has never been a colony, yet in *Old Phuket Town* you can definitely sense a colonial atmosphere. A stroll through this old quarter reveals many historic buildings in the Sino-Portuguese style. In Soi Rommani you will find one little gem after another → p. 67

● *Ride the waves*
A trip across the waves from beach to beach or to an offshore island is an essential part of a holiday in Phuket. On Rawai Beach a whole armada of *long-tails* awaits customers → p. 20

● *Breach the peace*
Buddhist monasteries are generally tranquil places in Thailand. In *Wat Chalong*, however, noise is part of the experience. Visitors set off chains of fireworks – to express gratitude for wishes fulfilled. You too can make a bang in the monastery, as the fireworks are sold on site → p. 59

● *Sail in the Andaman Sea*
The *Andaman Sea* is Asia's number one sailing region, and nowhere will you see more yachts at anchor than off Phuket. Go on board! On the noticeboards of restaurants and bars in the bays of Ao Sane and Chalong, and on Nai Harn Beach, sailors post offers of trips on their private boats → p. 92

● *Bar hopping*
The centre of nightlife in Phuket is *Soi Bangla on Patong Beach*. Hundreds of bars are lined up one next to the other, most of them no more than a counter with a roof above it. No other place in Thailand presents such a lively, uninhibited scene at night, with a carnival atmosphere wherever you look. And don't worry, women tourists too are welcome everywhere → p. 54

● *It doesn't hurt a bit*
They stick spikes and hooks into their bodies and feel no pain. Pilgrims at the *Vegetarian Festival* in Phuket Town have entered a trance. Visitors from the West can't exclude the possibility that it might hurt just to look (photo) → p. 99

ONLY IN

BEST OF ...

● *History lessons*
The history of Phuket was shaped by Chinese immigrants. When it's raining, why not head for the *Thaihua Museum*, a converted Chinese school, to find out where they came from and how they lived → p. 68

● *Learn to cook Thai*
Rock around the wok! In *Pum's Cooking School* on Patong Beach you can learn what makes the curry creamy and where the spice in prawn soup comes from → p. 52

● *Shop until you drop*
You can pass a whole rainy day in *Jungceylon* with ease. Phuket's biggest shopping centre with over 300 shops and a department store can entice even the anti-shopping brigade to join in a spree. And if you get hungry, refreshments are on offer at lots of restaurants (photo) → p. 53

● *Below ground*
It never rains here! The *Phuket Tin Mining Museum* is a reconstruction of working life underground, including life-size miners → p. 73

● *Old-fashioned splendour*
The *Thavorn Hotel* in Phuket Town has lost its stars one by one over the years. But its old-time lobby is still a wonderful place to spend a while when the weather is dull. No wonder part of it has been declared a 'museum' → p. 70

● *Meet the sharks*
There's no need to be afraid when you go eyeball to eyeball with the sharks. The glass tunnel through the *Phuket Aquarium* was built to be strong. You can also get close up to swarms of little coral fish → p. 61

RAIN

RELAX AND CHILL OUT
Take it easy and spoil yourself

● *Land of milk and honey*
Immerse yourself in the elegant world of the *Spa at the Marriott Resort* on Mai Khao Beach, bathing in milk and honey or an arrangement of sweet-scented flowers (photo). For two, it's twice as much fun. Couples can relax together with a romantic spa package → **p. 45**

● *Happy hour on the bay*
A mojito is always a good sundowner. Especially when you have a stunning view to go with it. On the quarterdeck of the *Royal Phuket Yacht Club*, for example, high above the bay of Nai Harn. During Happy Hour you get two drinks for the price of one → **p. 63**

● *(Almost) alone on the beach*
Yes, there are still beaches on Phuket where you can almost count the number of people on the fingers of one hand. Not many tourists find their way to the overgrown bay of *Hin Kruai*. You won't find more Robinson Crusoe feeling anywhere else on the island → **p. 47**

● *Chocolates in the marina*
The cappuccino chocolates melt in your mouth, and the raspberries on white chocolate are seasoned with a hint of chilli. At the *Watermark Patisserie* in the Boat Lagoon you can indulge your palate, and feast your eyes on the yachts in the marina → **p. 73**

● *Give your soul a holiday*
Simply close your eyes and let your thoughts run free like clouds in the sky. *Island Yoga* on Ko Yao Noi provides relaxation for body and soul with meditation and yoga → **p. 80**

● *Luxury on the beach*
Snow-white Kata Beach is wonderful just as it is. But why not add a bit of luxury? If that's what you like, the *Re Ka Ta Beachclub* is the right place. Comfortable sun loungers, light cuisine, many kinds of coffee – hot or iced. And if the sea is too salty for you, you can swim in the pool → **p. 43**

INTRODUCTION

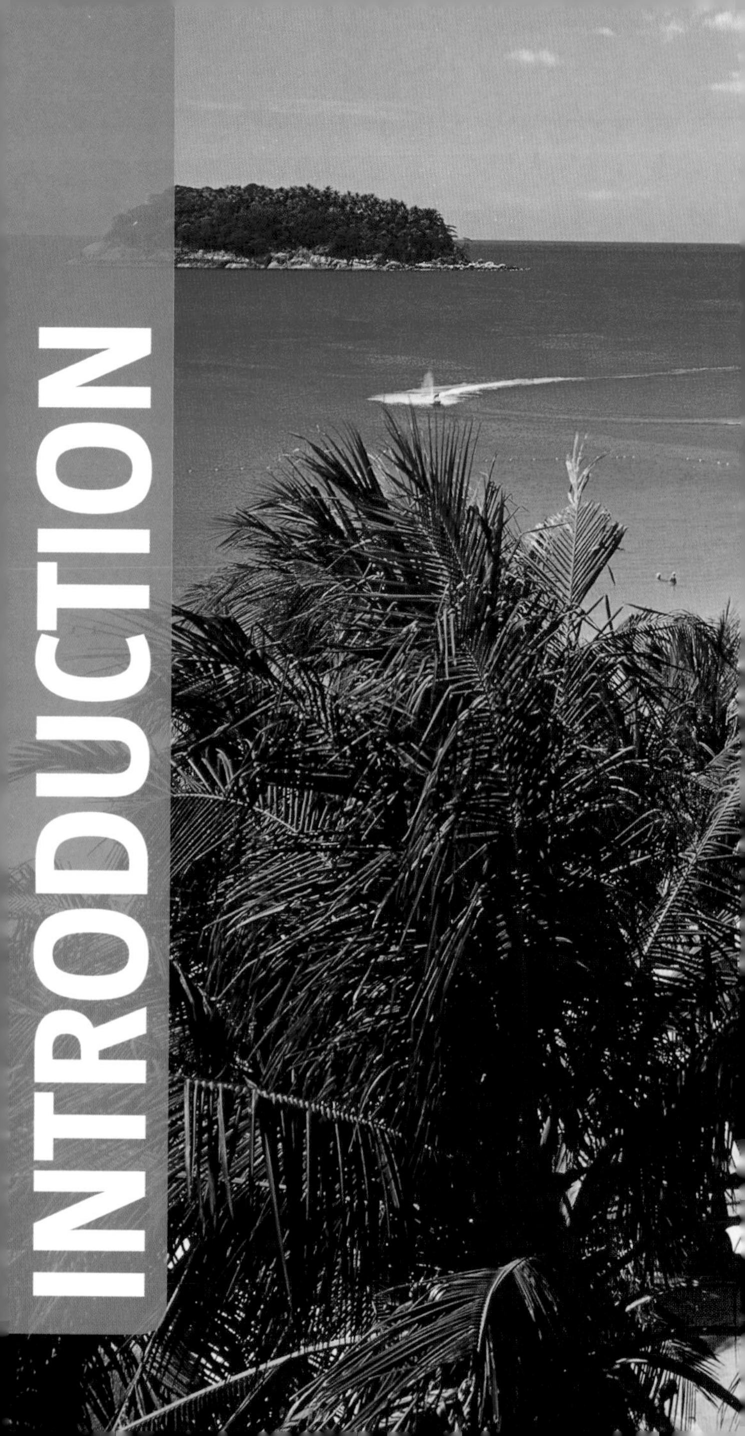

DISCOVER PHUKET!

Stunning beaches and jungle, colourful markets and gigantic shopping temples, a dizzy nightlife and an island capital where the old quarter is being transformed into a lively open-air museum – no wonder Phuket is such a popular holiday destination. The whole world comes here. The island draws more than five million tourists each year. The super-rich anchor their luxury yachts, and regular holidaymakers too relax on Phuket, having a good time and learning from the Thais that life is nicer when lived with a smile.

Saffron-coloured monks' robes glow in the light of the morning sun. In elaborately decorated temples, the faithful kneel in front of Buddha statues that gleam in gold, holding lotus flowers in their cupped hands. Fishermen tie brightly coloured cloths to the prow of their boats, and taxi drivers hang scented wreaths of jasmine and orchids from the rear-view mirrors of their chugging tuk tuks, four-wheeled mini taxis. All of this is intended to attract good fortune and ward off evil, whether on sea or land. Rubber trees stand in straight rows on extensive plantations, coconut palms

Photo: Kata Yai Beach

Playful lightness: a reclining Buddha at the Wat Sirey temple near Phuket Town

cast feathery shadows on the snow-white and golden-yellow beaches. In little bays, corals grow almost up to the shore of fine-grained sand. The sea stretches away to the horizon like a carpet of cornflower blue. When you dive in, it's like swimming in a gigantic aquarium. You can almost reach out and stroke fish that are as colourful as confetti. All the bright shades of the tropics! Above and below water, this island is a feast for the eyes.

Fish as colourful as confetti, almost close enough to touch

Phuket is Thailand's biggest island: 48 km/30 miles long, 22 km/14 miles wide. With a total surface area of 543 km²/209 sq miles (by way of comparison: the city state of Singapore has an area of 640 km²/247 sq miles), it is also the second-smallest of the kingdom's 76 provinces. In terms of its economy, the country's most important holiday destination has a leading position. Only in Bangkok, the capital city and in-

1518
The Portuguese found the first trading post for tin

1681
King Narai appoints French missionary René Charbonneau to be governor of Phuket

1785
Burmese invaders besiege Thalang, then the capital city. Thai women dress as soldiers and the Burmese retreat, believing they are outnumbered

1809–1812
Burmese forces land on Phuket three times, burn down Thalang and massacre the inhabitants

dustrial centre of Thailand, 860 km/535 miles away, is the average level of earnings higher than on Phuket. By Thai standards, many of the 340,000 inhabitants are quite affluent. They no longer live in wooden houses on piles but in dwellings made of bricks and mortar. They go to work on a motorbike or in their own car. However, it was not international tourism that first triggered a construction boom on Phuket and filled the streets with motorbikes. In Thailand, this island of tin miners, fishermen and rubber planters was always regarded as a rich place, even before the first backpackers came from far-away Europe in the 1970s and stayed in huts made of palm fronds on lonely beaches.

The first rubber trees were planted on Phuket in 1903, but even before this an activity that earned many millions had changed the face of the island: tin mining. The spread of industrialisation in Europe in the 19th century caused a rapid increase in the demand for tin. Thousands of Chinese labourers came from Malaysia to Phuket to work in the mines. Today about a quarter of the population is of Chinese origin. As late as 1977 the island earned twice as much from tin as from tourism. The decline in extraction began only with a fall in the price of tin in the 1980s.

The ancestors of the Muslim fishermen, too, once came from Malaysia as day labourers. Along with the Chinese and the ethnic Thais, who immigrated from southern China to what is now Thailand about a thousand years ago, they are proud *Khon Phuket*, citizens of Phuket, who all get along together peacefully. Only one small group continues to lead a marginal existence: the *Chao Leh* (literally: sea people, also known as sea gypsies). They are among the first people who settled on the shores of Phuket, but their origins are an enigma to ethnographers to this day.

1897
The first school is opened

1903
The first rubber-tree saplings are planted

1906
First floating tin-extraction platform off Phuket

1950
First bridge to the mainland

1976
Opening of the international airport

1980–1990
Building boom on Patong Beach

2001
Construction work on the last untouched beach

This history of a multicultural society is also evident in the places of worship on Phuket. Muslim Thais pray facing Mecca in a whitewashed mosque. Buddhist Thais put their hands together in prayer in a *wat*, a brightly coloured temple with an almost playful lightness of character. No less colourful, and adorned with dragons' heads too, are the Chinese temples *(sanjao)*, under whose red roofs both Buddhist and Taoist ceremonies are held.

In Phuket Town, several magnificent residences in the Sino-Portuguese style of architecture with artistically designed balustrades and columns, stucco façades and round-headed windows serve as reminders of the wealth held by tin and rubber magnates in days gone by. With 70,000 residents, Phuket Town is the administrative and historic centre of the island. However, some tourists don't make it into town even if their holiday lasts several weeks – because they simply don't want to leave the beaches.

There are of course other islands in Southeast Asia for holidaymakers to lie in warm sand, but nowhere else do they find some twenty beaches of high quality, as on Phuket. And what is a dream beach for one person might be someone else's nightmare. However, this is part of the charm of Phuket: it has beaches for peace and quiet, or for lots of noise and action. Those who are so inclined can lie down with crowds of others beneath a forest of sunshades, for example on Patong Beach, and dance the night away to disco music in 1001 bars. Or, for example at the south end of Bang Tao Beach, they can watch fishermen pulling the day's catch out of their little boats. Here, the music at night is played by cicadas, and the nightlife is mainly confined to gazing at stars in the sky.

Phuket has bustling beaches – and quiet ones too

Phuket is a real pearl, one of the most attractive holiday destinations in Southeast Asia. All traces of the tsunami in 2004 were removed long ago. The same applies to other holiday destinations in southern Thailand. Ferries plough through the waves on the 90-minute trip to the two islands of Phi Phi, two tiny sisters that possess a dramatic natural beauty. Tall as skyscrapers, limestone rocks rise vertically above beaches of white sand to be reflected in clear water. This stunning scenery attracts

2004
A tsunami causes the deaths of 5395 people, including 2436 foreign tourists, in southern Thailand. 250 people die on Phuket

2007
The number of visitors to Phuket reaches the five-million mark for the first time

2010
Major investments in Phuket's infrastructure: the government makes 340 million euros available for roads, expanding the airport and the exhibition centre

2012
The Siam Niramit cultural theatre puts on shows with 150 performers on a mega-stage

Beach volleyball on Ko Phi Phi: falling over on sand as fine as icing sugar presents no problem really

crowds of visitors. Since Leonardo DiCaprio came here for the filming of The Beach, Ko Phi Phi has become a party island. Tourist advertising likes to describe it as one of the ten most beautiful islands in the world. When you push your way through the masses of visitors in the cramped village on the island, you may have your doubts about this, but outside the main settlement there are quiet spots on Phi Phi where you can enjoy the natural splendour in peace – above and below the water, as the island and the islets around it are a paradise for divers.

For an truly quiet holiday, head for another pair of sister islands lying close to Phuket: Ko Yao Noi and Ko Yao Yai, both of them green

An oasis of green times two: Ko Yao Noi and Ko Yao Yai

oases in the sea, as they are still largely covered by jungle. The locals earn a living mainly from catching fish and tapping rubber trees, and tourists are few and far between. If you like riding a bike through lush vegetation, doing yoga, watching hornbill birds or simply hanging out in a hammock and feeling at peace, these are the perfect islands. On the Yao Islands you get an impression of how things were on Phuket before visitors from overseas came in droves. Here you are in territory that has hardly opened up to tourism – so no bars, loungers on the beach or advertising in several languages.

Phuket and the islands confront you with extremely pleasant choices. Whether you prefer peace or action, a stage show or natural beauty – the island world of the Andaman Sea has it all. It is never far to the nearest beach – and visitors are met with a friendly smile.

1 Style on the plate

Eye-catchers Those little extras on the edge of a plate often earn admiration. Why not learn for yourself how to make edible art from carrots, melons or radishes? At Pat's fruit-styling course *(Pat's Home Thai Cooking 26/4 Kwang Road, Phuket)* or the *Phuket Thai Cookery School (39/4 Thepatan Rd., Phuket Town)* you can learn how to make fruit and vegetables look like flowers in just a few hours. *Phuket Easytour (www.phuketeasytour.com)* organises cooking courses once a week, including the art of cutting food into shapes.

Ride the waves 2

Surfing The west of Phuket and especially Kata Beach are becoming popular with surfers. *Surf Shop Nautilus (www.surfinphuket.com)* and *Phuketsurf (www.phuketsurf.com)* cater for them, while the *Ska Bar* and *The Tube* are the places to hang out and relax after coming out of the water. For those who want more than a board, the *Phuket Surf School (www.salt water-dreaming.com)* on Surin Beach is the place to take surfing lessons.

3 Eggs and shells

Animal rights European standards of animal welfare still often seem alien to Thais. But awareness of the issue is increasing! The best proof of this is the *Turtle Foundation (photo)* at the *JW Marriott Phuket Resort*, which provides information and practical help. Turtles' nests are guarded, or taken to the incubation and breeding station of the institute for marine biology at *Phuket Aquarium*. Another project at the *Aleenta Resort (Natai, www.aleenta.com)* trains local people as turtle guards.

Among the treetops

Sleep aloft A good view is guaranteed from the rustic tree houses of the *Tree Tops Jungle Safari (123 Moo. 6, Klong Sok, www.treetops.co.th, photo)*. The accommodation is built on tall piles and accessed by steps. Guests have a view of the Khao Sok National Park, which is close enough to touch here: some of the huts have a tree growing through them. A different kind of tree house can be found at the *Angsana Laguna Phuket Kids Club (Bang Tao Bay, www.angsana.com)*. It is brightly coloured and keeps young holidaymakers happy and occupied with games and crafts while their parents relax. There is even a tree-house café with healthy meals for kids.

New uses

Recycling The idea of recycling is slowly but surely catching on – in the art scene, for example. Somrak Maneemai uses driftwood, scraps of metal and glass to make attractive works of art that fit into your luggage for the journey home. They are on display at the *Red Gallery (Soi Naya 2, Rawai)*. Local bars and restaurants have also taken to the recycled look. At fashionable *Brush restaurant (Kalim Beach, Patong, www.brushphuket.com, photo)*, the walls are panelled with old wood, and all sorts of curiosities and knick-knacks create a nice ambience. Perhaps some of the items came from the *Recycled Art Fair (www.myseek.org)*, which is organised by the local SEEK organisation promoting sustainability.

IN A NUTSHELL

ENVIRONMENT

The biggest asset for a holiday island like Phuket is an intact environment. However, the construction boom caused by tourism has had severe effects on the natural environment. The water table is falling, energy consumption is rising, and over five million holiday guests per year create a huge amount of waste. Beach resorts operators were the first to recognise how important it is to protect the environment – and how they themselves can save money. It is now normal for them to ask guests not to demand a change of towels every day. It is also normal for air conditioning to be switched off automatically when guests leave their rooms.

The enormously high consumption of plastic bags is a particular problem on Phuket, as in the rest of Thailand. Even the smallest purchases are placed in plastic bags at shop checkouts without asking or thinking about it. In February 2012 the provincial government initiated an "Anti Plastic Bag" campaign on Phuket and started to distribute 840,000 shopping bags made of fabric, but old habits die hard. It is still the exception rather than the rule to see locals or holidaymakers go shopping with a basket or textile bag. At the countless cooked-food stalls on the streets, the meals are normally packed in plastic or styrofoam boxes to carry away, and this packaging is often thrown on the ground by the side of the road or on the beach. These bad habits in respect to litter are not only caused by lack of environmental awareness – there

Photo: Kao Phra Thaeo National Park

Longtails and mangrove swamps, Buddhism and prostitution – Phuket is an island with many faces

is also a shortage of bins in places where many people come together.

FALANG

When Thais speak of *falang* (sometimes it is written *farang*, because the R is pronounced like an L), they are referring to all pale-skinned foreigners. The origin of the expression is possibly a corruption of the word *foreigner*.

LONGTAIL

A longtail is not some kind of monkey,

but an open motor boat that can often be seen in coastal waters in southern Thailand. These high-prowed wooden boats get their name (in Thai: hang yao) from special outboard motors. The propeller, which looks like the tuft at the end of a long tail, is attached to a shaft about 1.5 m/4.5 ft in length and is lowered into the water behind the boat. Longtails were once only used by fishermen, but now they often take tourists on trips along the coast or to offshore islands. As they make a loud droning noise, it is best

MANGROVES

They form coastal jungles and a species-rich ecosystem: mangrove forests act as a nursery for young fish, crabs and prawns. Their roots provide a natural breakwater against the waves and protect the land from erosion. The shallow, muddy east coast provides ideal conditions for the growth of mangroves. They have always been felled here to make charcoal – which has not on the whole damaged the environment. In recent times trees have been felled on a much larger scale, to make way for large prawn farms. However, the importance of intact mangrove forests for the environment has now been understood. In 2012 the government in Bangkok approved an investment of nearly 6.5 million dollars to build a road on the east coast. In order to give as much protection as possible to a mangrove forest near Phuket Town, this road is being built on stilts. The prime minister came in person to be informed about the project on the spot.

MONARCHY

Since the coup of 1932, Thailand has been a parliamentary democracy, but the royal dynasty, and King Bhumibol Adulyadej, Rama IX, in particular is held in high esteem. The king avoids intervention in day-to-day politics, but no-one can govern without his consent. His wishes are regarded as commands.

MONKEYS & MORE

Only seven per cent of the area of Phuket is now jungle. The largest area of uninterrupted forest is the *Kao Phra Thaeo Wildlife Park* in the northeast of the island. This nature reserve covering 22 km²/8.5 sq miles is inhabited by porcupines, wild boar and dwarf deer, but visitors seldom catch sight of these animals. Gibbons and macaque monkeys,

Colourful mini-temple: a place to make offerings to the spirits

to bring some ear plugs or look out for a boat that has a silencer fitted to the engine. You can charter a longtail boat, but only if you hire the captain too. This makes sense, as the swivel outboard motors mounted horizontally take some getting used to. You will find a hang yao on most tourist beaches on Phuket. A whole armada of them awaits passengers on the ● beach of Rawai (see p. 64).

which are also extremely shy, swing through the boughs of the trees, and sometimes a hornbill bird can be seen circling above the jungle. Cobras and pythons slither through the undergrowth, and not only in the wildlife park. Yet as these reptiles keep well out of the way of humans, their greatest enemies, most visitors see them only at the snake farm in Chalong. The tigers, leopards and elephants that once lived wild on Phuket were hunted to extinction or robbed of their habitat long ago. Sea turtles are becoming ever rarer, but each year in December and January some of these ancient survivors of evolution dig big holes on the beaches of Nai Yang and Mai Khao in order to lay eggs the size of pingpong balls. There is a greater variety of marine fauna. The waters around Phuket are excellent for diving thanks to a fascinating underwater world in which species ranging from coral-reef fish to whale sharks can be discovered.

Plant life on Phuket, like its fauna, has suffered severely from extensive agriculture and the extraction of tin. Coconut palms, casuarina trees with their long needles, and rubber trees, planted in parallel rows as straight as a die, can be seen all over the island. One rare kind of palm is called *Lahng Khao*. Its leaves have black veins and its undersides are whitish in colour. The species is known only from the *Kao Phra Thaeo nature reserve* and the *Khao Sok National Park* on the mainland in southern Thailand. Visitors can admire the species-rich ecosystem of the mangrove swamps without getting their feet wet by taking a stroll on the raised boardwalks in *Sirinat National Park* in the northwest of the island.

PROSTITUTION

The number of prostitutes in Thailand is estimated at between 200,000 and 800,000. By offering their services in public, prostitutes risk a fine of up to 1000 baht. Those who engage the services of under-age prostitutes (i.e. those below the age of 18), can be given a prison sentence of up to 20 years. In the last few years, the police have increased efforts to combat child prostitution. Offenders can also be sentenced by courts in their country of origin. Many underage prostitutes were enticed to Thailand from Burma, Laos and southern China with the promise of a job. The centre of the sex business on Phuket is Patong Beach. In hundreds of bars so-called bar girls wait for customers to buy them a drink and take them back to their room for a night. It is not unusual for such liaisons to end with marriage and immigration to the holidaymaker's home country. Most

Rubber mats on the line: the rubber has to dry for several days

of the women who work in this way come from the poor northeast of Thailand. As sex workers they hope for earnings that they could never achieve from employment in factories, for example. Nevertheless they are offended if they are described as prostitutes.

RELIGION

Almost three quarters of the residents of Phuket are Buddhists (the proportion for Thailand as a whole is 95 present), and one quarter are Muslims. It

were carried out to sea by rip tides. These currents beneath the surface are like rivers in the sea. They can occur even when the waves are not big. The local authorities have erected warning signs in seven languages on the west coast and emphasise that red flags on the beaches are a sign of real danger and should on no account be ignored.

RUBBER TREES

Originally brought over from Brazil, rubber trees today grow in neat lines all

Lighting joss sticks: for the Thais, rituals of sacrifice are part of everyday religious life

is rare to see women wearing veils. The religions coexist without any problems. Many young Buddhist men enter a monastery for a few weeks to live as monks.

RIP CURRENTS

Especially in the monsoon season, between May and October or November, the sea on the west coast of Phuket can become a death trap for tourists. At the start of the monsoon in 2012, six holidaymakers drowned within four weeks. They

over southern Thailand. In the 19th century the English smuggled the seeds of rubber trees from Brazil and introduced them in Singapore. It was the governor of Trang in southern Thailand who first ordered the planting of young rubber trees on Siamese soil in 1901. From there, the plantations spread quickly. In 1903 the rubber boom began on Phuket. Today Thailand is the world's largest producer. Harvesting rubber is an extremely labour-intensive process. Long before sunrise, the rubber tappers slit open the bark with a sickle-shaped knife in the light of lamps attached to their foreheads. The white resin drips into a halved coconut shell attached to the tree via a small channel. After a few hours the raw rubber can then be collected. Following treatment with acid, it is compressed into mats in a device like a laundry mangle. The mats are hung on frames to dry for a few days, before being processed to make tyres and condoms, swimming shoes and erasers in factories in Thailand and abroad.

SEA PEOPLE

The so-called sea gypsies call themselves *Chao Leh*, sea people. They were long feared as pirates, but today only a few thousand live on Phuket and several other islands in the Andaman Sea. They are small in stature, have almost black skin and curly hair. Their origins are unknown. According to one theory they are descended from the Negritos who live on the Andaman and Nicobar islands, which belong to India. Although the term sea gypsies is applied to all three ethnic groups (Moken, Moklen, Urak Lawoi), only the Moken, of whom there are several hundred, are true maritime nomads who live off what the sea provides: pearls, corals, shells and fish. The other two ethnic groups have remained fishermen and gatherers, but have now settled down. Members of the Urak Lawoi live in two poor villages on Ko Sirey and on the beach at Rawai. If you would like to support them, you can buy fish from them – but not corals, as the sale of coral is prohibited.

SPIRIT HOUSES

They look like miniature temples, standing on platforms in front of houses, shops, hotels and banks – in fact they can be seen everywhere, because spirits can lurk in any place, and these colourful little temples are intended to give them a home. Belief in spirits *(phii)* is deeply rooted in Thai society, and is older than Buddhism. With offerings such as flowers, a bowl of rice or a glass of water, the Thais try to gain the favour of their invisible neighbours and prevent them from wandering around. It can never do any harm to greet the spirits. Many Thais put their hands together in a *wai* (see below) when they pass the more conspicuous spirit houses, and if they are driving, they sound the horn of the car. You can hear a great deal of hooting when you drive from Phuket Town to Patong Beach, passing the big spirit house on Patong Hill on the left-hand side.

WAI

Thais greet each other not with a handshake but with a *wai.* This involves putting their hands together in front of the chest, with the finger tips pointing upwards. This sounds simpler than it really is, as a *wai* is not only a gesture of greeting. It is also a way of saying thank you, asking for forgiveness or showing respect to someone else. The question of how high the hands are held and who performs the *wai* first is of significance here. People of lower social standing greet their superiors first, and young persons greet older persons first. The highest-held *wai* with finger tips above a deeply bowed head is reserved for the royal family and monks. No Thai will hold it against a tourist if the *wai* is not performed quite correctly. It is best to use this gesture sparingly, and not for example try it out on the hotel staff. In response to a *wai* it suffices to nod the head slightly. To respond to a beggar's *wai* is to make yourself a laughing stock.

FOOD & DRINK

Culinary treats on Phuket are as international as the visitors to the island. Here you can get fish and chips, pizza or paella. But if you are planning a journey of gastronomic discovery, don't fail to try the light, fresh and aromatic cooking of the Thais.

The sounds of steaming and sizzling come from little eateries on every corner. Mobile food stalls park by the side of the road, the cook places a few stools and small tables on the pavement, and hey presto! – you have an open-air restaurant serving noodle soup with chicken or duck, fried rice with prawns or sweet pancakes with pineapple for just a few baht.

Thailand's low-fat food is so healthy that nutritionists love it. Red meat is used in small quantities, while poultry and sea food are eaten more often – with plenty of herbs and spices. Vegetables are cooked briefly so that they stay crisp and keep their vitamins. Thai cuisine is also perfectly adapted to the tropical climate. Meals spiced up with chilli provide protection against bacteria and are good for the circulation, which can be affected by the high humidity. The food is light and easy to digest.

Thai dishes are served in bite-sized pieces, and eaten holding a spoon in the right hand. Only dishes with noodles – including soup! – are served with chopsticks. A typical Thai menu can consist of courses with up to five different kinds of flavours. Their combination stimulates the taste buds, and is accompanied by a big bowl

Photo: Shrimps with rice and hot red sauce

Made in heaven, and as hot as hell – Thai food is not only light and healthy, but absolutely delicious

of rice. All the diners help themselves. It is considered impolite to heap up all the items onto your plate at once.

Only higher-class restaurants have fixed times for *lunch* (11.30am–2pm) and dinner (6.30pm–10pm).

On Phuket, as everywhere in the south of Thailand, the taste of neighbouring Malaysia is ever present. One example is *gaeng massaman*, a red curry with beef, peanuts and chunks of potato. Inhabitants of an island are extremely keen on sea food, of course. However, the coastal waters have been overfished, and the famous *Phuket lobster* (not actually a lobster but a kind of langoustine) usually comes from a fish farm. Its smaller relatives, prawns and shrimps *(gung),* are almost all produced on the farms that have been established along many stretches of the coast and on Phuket itself.

Thais love hot, spicy food. In tourist restaurants the use of chilli is more sparing, but if you are concerned about spicy food, order a dish with the words *mai peht* (not

LOCAL SPECIALITIES

▶ **gaeng kiau wan gai** – This green curry with chicken and aubergines is a delicacy to make you sweat. Slightly sweet *(wan)*

▶ **gung hom pa** – Prawns in batter. You dip them in tartare sauce or in a sweet-sour vinegar with chilli rings (photo left)

▶ **kao pat** – Fried rice may not be haute cuisine, but it is a filling meal – made with egg *(kai)* and vegetables *(pak)*. Other ingredients that can be added are shrimps *(gung)*, pork *(mu)* or chicken *(gai)*

▶ **kui tiao nam** – This noodle soup is Thailand's favourite snack. Food stalls make it on every corner. Usually with pork *(mu)* or chicken, but it tastes particularly good with duck *(pet)*

▶ **plamuk tohd katiam pik thai** – Pieces of squid fried with garlic and pepper (not hot), always a tasty snack

▶ **pla piau wan** – This sauce with sweet and sour fried fish is served with a lot of colourful vegetables and pieces of pineapple

▶ **som tam** – Salad made from thin strips of green papaya with cocktail tomatoes, dried shrimps, small crabs and lots of chilli. Raw vegetables, sticky rice and charcoal-grilled chicken *(gai pat)* go well with it

▶ **tom kha gai** – This soup of chicken in coconut milk is an exotic treat. Beware: there are entire chilli pods in the spicy liquid

▶ **tom yam gung** – This sour prawn soup is Thailand's unofficial national dish. It gets its unmistakable taste from lemongrass, and its spiciness from chilli. Always eaten with rice

▶ **yam wunsen** – Salad of glass noodles with herbs, shrimps and minced pork. Chilli adds heat (photo right)

hot). Standards such as fried rice and noodle soup are usually seasoned by the guests themselves, using coarse chilli powder, sugar or a sweet-and-sour vinegar in which pieces of fresh chilli float. *Nam pla* (fish sauce) is used instead of salt. When chopped chilli is added, the fish sauce is known as *pik nam pla*. Take care with the quantity!

Side salads in the Western style, for example with lettuce or tomatoes, are not eaten by the Thais. A typical Thai salad *(yam)* is more of a dish in itself and is often eaten between main meals. It is almost always hot, especially the filling *yam nüa*, a salad with a sour taste made from strips of beef garnished with garlic, coriander, onions and powdered chilli. A popular dish known as *yam wunsen* has glass noodles as the main ingredient.

Thais love sweet treats – the sweeter the better. Small, home-made, mega-calorie creations in all colours of the rainbow can be bought from stalls at festivities, markets and on the street. One delicious snack that is not extremely sweet is sticky rice cooked in coconut milk, which today is still served prettily wrapped in banana leaves. Visitors to Phuket can sample all the fruit of the tropics. The locals consider *durian* to be the queen of fruits. It is also known as stinkfruit, for a good reason. The yellowish-white flesh within the prickly outer skin has a creamy softness. Either you can't resist it, or it makes you shudder. By contrast everyone likes a mango *(ma-muang)*, which tastes extremely good with concentrated coconut milk and sticky rice *(kao niau)*. The Thais also love strips of green mango, which they dunk in a mixture of sugar and chilli. Beneath the thick, wine-red skin of the mangosteen *(mangkut)* is a white flesh that tastes sweet and a little bit sour at the same time. It is also worth trying a hairy rambutan *(ngo)*, a delicious lychee *(linchi)* or the red Java apple *(jompu)*. The availability of freshly pressed fruit juice is mostly limited to orange juice – which is often diluted with lemonade. Other thirst-quenchers are water *(nam bau)* and mineral water, as well as a variety of soft drinks. The most popular local brands of beer are *Singha* and *Chang*, and international brands such as *Heineken* and *Tiger* are also brewed in Thailand. Imported European beer is sold in many bars.

A cheap spirit named mekhong is distilled from rice, and sometimes described as 'whisky'. Saeng som (made from sugar cane) is more expensive and has a less perfumed flavour, but this one

Thais know that the appearance of a meal is important

too should not be drunk neat. With soda water and a shot of lime juice it makes an iced long drink. Tourists like to mix it with cola.

SHOPPING

Almost everything that is sold on Phuket comes from other parts of the country and is relatively expensive. If you are also visiting Bangkok or Chiang Mai in north Thailand, you should make your purchases there. The best places for shopping on Phuket are the island's capital and Patong Beach. Environmentalists advise you not to buy shells and corals. Shellfish are taken alive out of the sea and boiled to get the shells, while trading in corals is prohibited.

ANTIQUES

Trustworthy shops will draw your attention to the fact that an export permit is required for antiques, and will obtain one for you. If you do it yourself, the procedure can be complicated. Information is available from the National Museum in Thalang *(tel. 076 3114 26)*.

BUDDHA STATUES

The Thai customs authorities are particularly sensitive if they discover Buddha statues in tourists' luggage. Even the cheapest plastic Buddhas may not be exported without a permit! Only amulets to be worn on the body may be taken out

of the country. You can apply for an export permit at the National Museum in Thalang – so long as it is not for a statue of historic value, which may not be exported at all.

CLOTHING

Every other shop near the beaches seems to be a tailor. Arrange for at least two fitting sessions and be sure to have alterations made if the clothes do not fit. The largest selection of ready-made clothes is available from *Patong Beach*, the *Central Festival* shopping centre and the *Robinson department store* in Phuket Town. In some textile shops in town (e.g. in *Thalang Rd.*) you will find the typical Thai cloth that is called *pa kao ma*. Worn as a short sarong in rural areas, it can also be used as a sash, shawl, head covering or towel. This all-purpose cloth usually comes in a red-and-blue or red-and-white check pattern. It fades when washed frequently, but becomes softer. Batik cloths are also made on Phuket, so you can take all the bright colours of the tropics home with you for a modest price.

Spices, clothes, gold and antiques –
while Phuket is not exactly a shoppers
paradise, you will find souvenirs here

GOLD

Gold jewellery of up to 23 carats is sold
in special gold shops (not at the other
jewellers!), which can be recognised by
their red interior fittings. Prices depend
on the current price of gold. This high-
quality jewellery can be resold, possibly
at a profit if the price of gold rises. The
best choice of gold jewellery is to be had
in Phuket Town.

JEWELS AND PEARLS

Be extremely careful when buying pre-
cious stones. Don't let touts persuade
you to go into a shop, and never buy
from street traders. Phuket is one of the
leading places for buying pearls. To find
out how to tell the difference between
real and artificial ones, visit a pearl farm
(e.g. on the island of Naka Noi, to which
you can book a trip at a travel agent).

PAINTINGS

A Picasso for about 40 dollars? No problem, you can have one – not an original,
but a masterly copy. In Phuket's tourist
centres a number of local artists have
specialised in copying the work of their
world-famous colleagues. Holidaymakers can have their portrait painted without having to sit for hours – a passport
photo is all you need. Original Thai paintings by Thai artists are sold at the galler-
ies in the old quarter of Phuket Town.

SPICES

Pepper or cinnamon, chilli, curcuma or
curry paste – exotic spices cost only a
fraction of the price you would pay at
home. All the big supermarkets, Tesco
Lotus for example, are extremely well
stocked. Prices are lowest at the market
in Phuket Town.

THE PERFECT ROUTE

BREAKFAST BY THE SEA, BUDDHAS IN THE HILLS

Start your trip where others anchor their boats. The bay of ❶ *Chalong* → p. 58 is a natural harbour for yachts and a meeting place for sailors from all over the world. While enjoying a hearty farmer's breakfast with sautéed potatoes at the lighthouse at the end of the road to the left of the pier, you have a panoramic view of the bay and all the boats. You can even take a stroll through the fleet of sailing boats: the pier is 700 m/800 yd long and goes far out into the water. After that drive from the roundabout to the pier and take the second road on the right in the direction of the airport. After approx. 1 km/half a mile, a turn-off to the ❷ *Big Buddha* → p. 59 is signposted. This Enlightened One stands tall at 45 m/150 feet on a 400 m/1300-ft hill and faces east, looking straight towards the bay of Chalong. You have a fantastic, far-ranging view here. Back on the main road, it is worth making a detour north to ❸ *Wat Chalong* → p. 59 (photo left), the island's biggest monastery. Take a walk through the monastery grounds before returning to the roundabout and continuing on the 4021 in the direction of ❹ *Phuket Town* → p. 66. When you arrive, you can shop and stroll in Thalang Road and its side street Soi Rommani in the historic quarter. A lot of old houses with shops in the Sino-Portuguese style make this district attractive, and at the China Inn you will get an excellent meal in a beautifully restored townhouse.

HISTORY AND GIBBONS

Take Highway 402 towards the airport as far as the Heroines Monument, then turn right onto road no. 4027 and follow it to the ❺ *Thalang National Museum* → p. 37. Here you can learn all about the history of Phuket. Continue on the 4027 heading north, and after approx. 7 km/4.5 miles turn off into the jungle of the ❻ *Kao Phra Thaeo* → p. 36 nature reserve (signposted, photo right). The Gibbon Rehabilitation Centre explains how these primates are prepared for a life in the wild.

TIME FOR THE BEACH IN THE WEST

Back on the highway going north, cross the green interior of Phuket via Bang Rong village, turn left toward the airport after approx. 2 km/1.25 miles, and drive on to ❼ *Nai Yang Beach* → p. 47. Stretch out on the mats beneath the casuarina trees and treat yourself to some fresh grilled fish. Between May and November it gets quite windy here, and if you feel so inclined, you can take lessons in kite surfing. A few miles south of Nai Yang lies the wonderful beach of **8** *Nai Thon* → p. 46. Now is the time for a dip in the blue sea, and perhaps a massage on the beach afterwards. This is the place to get away from all the bustle – and if you like things even quieter, park approx. 2 km/1.25 miles south of Nai Thon by the side of the road above the bay of **9** *Hin Kruai* → p. 47. Look out for the signpost to 'Banana Beach'. A little path leads down to this superb beach.

SUSHI AT SURIN

The narrow coast road now bends into the island's interior again. Take road no. 4030 and then 4025, always heading south, as far as **10** *Surin Beach* → p. 56. Nowhere on Phuket will you find more top open-air restaurants right on the beach. How about some sushi and sashimi in the Catch Beach Club?

EVENING ACTION

When the sun goes down, make your way to **11** *Patong Beach* → p. 50, 13 km/8 miles south of Surin. The touristic heart of Phuket is one big show – and you have to have seen it! Stroll through the zone of bars on Soi Bangla, which is pedestrianised in the evening. Don't be too hesitant, as whole families with their children and all their belongings push through the crowds here. If you still have the energy for a shopping spree, then go to Jungceylon, the island's largest retail centre with 300 shops, where you can browse to your heart's content until 11 pm.

100 km/60 miles. 2.5 hours driving time.
Recommended duration: 1 day
Detailed map of the route on the back cover, in the road atlas and the pull-out map.

THE WEST COAST

What a coast! Green hills shelter beaches that go on for miles and small bays from the rest of the world. Holidaymakers from all over the globe come here to find peace and quiet – or lots of activity. On the west coast, which measures 50 km/30 miles from north to south, Phuket is at its best. Nature has created top-class beaches here – with a total length of 35 km/22 miles – so this is where you'll find almost all the beach resorts, and where visitors come for the sun. Patong Beach is Phuket's tourist centre, a town by the sea where sun loungers are lined up several rows deep. The further north you go, the quieter things become, and you can still discover beaches and bays where the palms and other trees outnumber the sunshades.

BANG TAO BEACH

(114 A–B 2–3) *(ill C7)* **This 6 km/3.5 mile-long beach, fringed by palm trees and casuarinas, has always been in pristine condition, but until the 1980s its hinterland, ruined by tin mining, looked as barren as the moon.**

Enter the Laguna Project. The deserted tin mines were flooded and a green landscape of lagoons by the sea with seven high-class resorts was created. Nevertheless, outside this impressive oasis of luxury Bang Tao has remained largely authentic to this day. On the southern part of the beach you will find a small

Relaxation beneath palm trees or action into the small hours – everything is possible on the quiet bays and long beaches in the west

tourist village with shops and cafés. More expensive shops and restaurants are situated on the access road to the Laguna Resort.

At Choeng Thale further inland the life of the mainly Muslim population has hardly been changed at all by tourism. The people still work as fishermen, farmers and traders. For Friday prayers they all assemble at the Islamiya Mosque, the largest mosque on Phuket.

FOOD & DRINK

The over 30 restaurants in the seven Laguna Resorts will satisfy even gourmets with high expectations. On the beach in front of the resorts there are a number of open-air restaurants that specialise in seafood. For a romantic evening for two, the *Banyan Tree* on the lagoons organises INSIDER TIP sunset dinner cruises *(Sanya Rak)* in a longtail (book in advance). On Lagoon Road (leading to the Laguna Resorts) a lot of restaurants have been established, some of them of excellent quality.

BABYLON BEACH CLUB

This rustic but chic open-air restaurant is right on the beach. Roberto serves up eat goulash as well as a Thai curry and different kinds of bread to go with it. Barbecue all you can eat every Wednesday and Sunday. You can even play table football and pool here. Wine list. *Daily 10am–1am | tel. 0815 38 21 10 | Budget*

Motorcyclists in front of Phuket's largest mosque, the Islamiya Mosque in Choeng Thale

Thai and Italian food 'just the way mamma cooks'. *Daily 11am–10.30pm | between Amora Hotel and Laguna Beach Resort | tel. 0819 70 53 02 | www.babylonbeachclub.com | Moderate*

DEDOS

Pablo, who learned to cook from Bocuse, produces top-quality Mediterranean cuisine with Thai and Japanese touches. His breast of duck with sweet and sour tamarind sauce is delicious. Pick-up service. *Daily from 6pm | Lagoon Rd. | tel. 076 32 51 82 | www.dedos-restaurant.com | Expensive*

NOK & JO'S

Rustic style at the southern end of Bang Tao on the road to Surin. Here you can

TOTO RESTAURANT

Roberto's spaghetti vongole, calzone and tiramisu taste just as good as in Italy; the wine is imported from there too. *Daily from 5pm | Lagoon Rd. | tel. 076 27 14 30 | www.totophuket.com | Moderate–Expensive*

WATERMARK PATISSERIE

Exquisite bakery and patisserie with a big selection of bread, rolls, croissants, cakes and chocolates. You can also have breakfast here. *Daily 7am–5pm | Lagoon Rd. | tel. 076 27 14 30 | Budget*

SPORTS & ACTIVITIES

The Laguna Resorts offer water sports, tennis, golf and squash. At *Quest Laguna*

Adventure (tel. 076 32 40 62) there is a climbing wall that you can tackle with safety equipment. *Dusit Laguna (www. lagunaphuket.com)* hires out bikes and organises cookery courses. At the *Banyan Tree Phuket* you can learn batik painting or relax with meditation and tai chi. The facilities in the resorts are open to all guests of the Laguna complex.

ENTERTAINMENT

There are several bars and pubs in the tourist village and near the entrance to the Laguna Resorts, such as *Peppers Bar*. In the Irish pub *The Craic* live music is played every Sunday from 9.30pm.

WHERE TO STAY

ANDAMAN BANG TAO BAY RESORT

A cosy little resort with extremely tasteful cottages right on the beach and a small pool. *16 rooms | 82/9 Bang Tao Beach | tel. 076 27 02 46 | www.andamanbang taobayresort.com | Expensive*

BANGTAO VILLAGE RESORT

Well-kept holiday cottages with lots of greenery and a small pool. All rooms are equipped with air-conditioning, TV and refrigerator. Located in a quiet side street in the town, the resort is about a ten minutes' walk from the beach. *28 rooms | Srisoonthorn Rd. | tel. 076 27 04 74 | www.bangtaovillageresort. com | Expensive*

BANYAN TREE PHUKET

Elegant and exclusive houses, some with their own pool (9 x 13 m/30 x 45 ft) that you can almost dive into from your bed. Excellent spa (no medical staff) with sauna, massage, meditation, yoga, aromatherapy, pool with current. Definitely number one among the Laguna Resorts. *150 rooms | Bang Tao Beach | tel. 076 32 43 74 | www.banyantree.com/en/ phuket | Expensive*

DUSIT LAGUNA

Lagoons to the right, lagoons to the left, and in front the sparkling sea. *Dusit is*

⭐ **Wat Phra Nang Sang and Wat Phra Thong**
Pretty as a picture: two temples on the highway near Thalang, radiant with colourful murals and lots of gold → p. 37

⭐ **FantaSea**
Kamala: the imaginative show includes a herd of elephants → p. 38

⭐ **Viewpoint**
Three beaches lining the sea like pearls below you – the viewpoint at Kata gives you a fantastic view → p. 42

⭐ **Mom Tri's Kitchen**
A lovely garden restaurant with works of art, a sea view and culinary surprises → p. 43

⭐ **Trisara**
Luxurious but expensive: Phuket's best resort is a paradise of wood and marble, pools and sea views above a beach to die for → p. 44

⭐ **Simon Cabaret**
Gaudy transvestite revue with music, dance and comedy – 50 'ladies' in lavish costumes → p. 54

MARCO POLO HIGHLIGHTS

surrounded by tropical gardens like an island in a sea of green. The architecture and interior fittings were designed with attention to Thai style. *254 rooms | 390 Srisoonthorn Rd. | tel. 076 36 29 99 | www. dusit.com | Expensive*

PHUKET NATURE PLACE
The rooms in these bungalows on stilts are basic, but they have air-conditioning, a fridge and TV. One of the best-priced

Phuket *(tel. 076 36 23 00 | www.laguna phuket.com)*. For other information, for example about Kamala and Surin beaches, see *www.phuketgoldcoast.com*.

KAO PHRA THAEO PARK ☼
(115 D1–2) *(Ⓜ E5–7)*
10 km/6 miles northeast of the Laguna Resorts (via road no. 4030), the little

Glowing colours: murals in Wat Phra Nang Sang, the oldest temple on Phuket

places to stay in Bang Tao on the northern edge of town (about ten minutes' walk from the beach). *4 rooms | Srisoonthorn Rd. | tel. 076 27 13 76 | www. phuketnatureplace.com | Moderate*

Information on the Laguna complex (including the purchase of houses and apartments) is available from *Laguna*

town of *Thalang* lies on Highway 402. At the only crossroads in town a road branches off to the nature reserve of *Kao Phra Thaeo (admission 200 baht)*. A trail leads through the jungle to the *Ton Sai waterfall* and in a walk of two hours continues to the *Bang Pae waterfall* and the *Gibbon Rehabilitation Centre (daily 9am–4pm)*. Here gibbons are prepared for life in the wild *(www.gibbonproject.org)* and visitors can sponsor them. Only those gibbons which will not be released from captivity, due to their age or injuries, can be seen here.

THALANG NATIONAL MUSEUM AND HEROINES MONUMENT
(115 D3) (*∅ E7–8*)

12 km/7.5 miles east of Bang Tao, road no. 4025 leads to the *Heroines Monument*, which is situated in the middle of the intersection with Highway 402. It commemorates two sisters, Chan and Muk, who saved Phuket from destruction by the Burmese in 1785. They created the impression of a huge army by clothing all the women as soldiers and mobilising them alongside the men. Beyond the intersection on road no. 4027 on the right, the *Thalang National Museum* offers a small but well-conceived presentation of the history of Phuket. The exhibition includes prehistoric archaeological finds, items of everyday use, crafts and old weapons. *Daily 8.30am–4.30pm | admission 30 baht*

WAT PHRA NANG SANG/WAT PHRA THONG ★ (114 C1) (*∅ D6*)

Two temples situated on Highway 402 in Thalang are worth a visit. The elegant *Wat Phra Nang Sang* (after the crossing with road no. 4030 go right towards Phuket Town, approx. 6 km/4 miles from Bang Tao Beach) is the oldest on the island. It was built about 250 years ago, when Thalang was the capital of Phuket. Colourful murals relate the history of Phuket and the fall of Ayutthaya.
Wat Phra Thong (just before leaving town turn right towards the airport) is home to a ● Buddha figure covered with a thick layer of gold leaf which is the subject of legends. Only the upper part of the statue is above ground. It is said that anyone who tries to dig out the statue or shows disrespect towards it will die.

KAMALA BEACH

(114 A3–4) (*∅ B–C 8–9*) Tourism came late to this flat bay. In the village of the same name, which stretches far inland, life continues peacefully as it used to, but this village idyll is attracting more and more foreigners who come to live on Phuket and build fine houses for themselves here.

Although a full tourist infrastructure exists here, do not expect too much of the shopping and nightlife.

FOOD & DRINK

Lots of places along Beach Rd. specialise in seafood. *Charoen Seafood (Budget–Moderate)*, which belongs to the *Kamala Dreams* resort, always has plenty of customers. In Foxtail Plaza in a side street off Beach Rd. the *Buffalo Steak House (Moderate)* didn't get its name for nothing, and local dishes are served at the *Thai Sugar Hut (Budget)*. There is a wide choice on the INSIDER TIP Thai buffet and classical Thai dancing on Wednesdays from 7pm at *The Kamala (Moderate)* in the *Print Kamala* resort on Beach Rd. In the *Kamala Bakery (Budget)* on the main road you can order cakes and filled baguettes to go with your cappuccino.

KOKOSNUSS

For all fans of German sausages, Thomas from Nuremberg serves the speciality of his home town, as well as fresh bread with cheese and different kinds of cold sausage. A German buffet is served five nights a week. *Daily from 7am | Soi 7 (an alley off Beach Rd.) | tel. 0815 38 52 85 | www.phuketkokosnuss.com | Budget–Moderate*

ROCKFISH

A high standard of Thai cooking and a few Western dishes with a good view: this restaurant on the cliffs at the southern end of the beach has such delights as tuna marinated in chilli paste with herb salad and deep-fried goat's cheese with

Wonderland: FantaSea is a gigantic show complex

onion marmalade. *Daily from 8am | Beach Rd. | tel. 076 27 97 32 | www.rock fishrestaurant.com | Moderate–Expensive*

SHOPPING

In the *Kamala Center & Shopping* at the edge of the village on the Patong road, every day is market day – especially for the locals. The stalls sell more or less everything from flashlights and crockery to cheap clothes. And of course there are Thai snacks to keep you going between meals.

ENTERTAINMENT

FANTASEA ⭐

A show straight from a fairy tale, including a herd of trained elephants, is presented in an arena for 3000 spectators at the *FantaSea fun park*. It is definitely worth paying the fairly high admission price. For 300 baht per person guests are picked up from hotels all over Phuket in minibuses and taken home afterwards. *Admission 1500 baht, with an opulent dinner buffet 1900 baht | tel. 076 38 51 11 | www.phuket-fantasea.com*

WHERE TO STAY

You will find several guesthouses in the stretch between the main road and the beach, including the cosy *Sabina Guesthouse (9 rooms | Kamala Beach | tel. 076 27 95 44 | www.chezsabina-guesthouse. com | Budget)*, run by the helpful Mr Phitsanu. Basic, but with TV, fridge, air conditioning.

INSIDER TIP ▶ BAAN CHABA

Pleasant cottages with air conditioning and minibar in an attractive, green little complex. The beach is only a few paces away. *8 rooms | Kamala Beach | tel. 076 27 91 58 | www.baanchaba.com | Moderate*

THE CLUB

On the main road, approx. five minutes from the beach, this resort offers excellent value for money. Pleasant rooms with TV, small kitchen, air conditioning. Small pool. *22 rooms | Main Rd. | tel. 0818 93 49 11 | www.theclubphuket.com | Budget–Moderate*

KAMALA BEACH RESORT

The largest resort in Kamala, right on the beach. Extremely comfortable rooms with TV, minibar. Four pools. *414 rooms | Kamala Beach | tel. 076 27 95 80 | www. kamalabeach.com | Expensive*

INSIDER TIP PAPA CRAB

What was once a travellers' hostel has turned into a well-kept boutique resort with stylish rooms for non-smokers. Low-key design and words of wisdom to decorate the walls. Only two minutes from the beach. *10 rooms | Beach Rd. | tel. 076 38 53 15 | www.phuketpapacrab.com | Moderate*

KARON BEACH

 MAP ON PAGE 41
(116 A–B 3–4) (*ɷ C11–12*) **On this 4 km/2.5-mile-long beach, fringed with bushes and trees, it does not get crowded even in high season.**

Almost all the resorts along with the shops and restaurants are on the other side of the beach road, which does not have heavy traffic. A tourist village has sprung up in the north around the *Karon Centre* next to the roundabout *(Karon Circle)*. Along the beach road some remaining open spaces with palms and undergrowth ensure that Karon often seems almost deserted, even in high season. This is a good choice for those who like things neither too quiet nor too noisy.

FOOD & DRINK

The best-value seafood is served in the basic open-air restaurants at the south end of Karon near the football stadium and at the north end near the roundabout.

OLD SIAM RESTAURANT

Outstanding Thai food served on the terrace, or indoors, where diners sit on the floor to enjoy a *Kanthoke dinner* typical of northern Thailand, with the dishes served on low tables. On Wed and Sun at 8.50pm classical Thai dances are performed. In the *Thavorn Palm Beach Resort*. *Daily lunch/dinner | 128/10 Karon Rd. | tel. 076 39 60 90 | Moderate–Expensive*

ON THE ROCKS ☼

Pleasant open-air restaurant in the *Marina Cottage* resort on the rocky slope by the sea. The seafood and Thai dishes are every bit as good as the view. *Daily lunch/dinner | tel. 0 76 33 06 25 | Moderate–Expensive*

SPORTS & ACTIVITIES

You can hire a surfboard on the beach. Motor boats are available for water skiing. There are diving schools, and parasailing is also possible.

ENTERTAINMENT

Nightlife on Karon Beach is restricted to a few bars in the tourist village at the north end and in the middle of the beach.

WHERE TO STAY

KARON BEACH HOTEL

Pleasant boutique hotel on the edge of the tourist village. Air-conditioned rooms with refrigerator, TV and a small balcony. Cross the road and walk a few paces to get to the beach. *16 rooms | 224/12 Karon Rd. | near Karon Circle | tel. 076 36 93 18 | www.karonbeach-hotel.com | Moderate*

INSIDERTIP ▶ KARON CAFÉ INN
A pleasant guesthouse with good food. TV, refrigerator and air-conditioning in every room. Only 150 m/150 yd to the beach. *16 rooms | Soi Islandia Park Resort | tel. 076 39 62 17 | www.karoncafe. com | Moderate*

MARINA PHUKET RESORT
The grounds are so green that you almost feel you are in the jungle. High-class wooden bungalows with every amenity on a rocky headland that divides Karon from Kata Beach. The pool is small, but there is direct access to the beach. *89 rooms | 47 Karon Rd. | tel. 076 33 06 25 | www.marinaphuket.com | Expensive*

RAMADA PHUKET SOUTHSEA
Comfortable hotel built in a U-shape around the pool, with only the road separating it from the beach. *152 rooms | 204 Karon Rd. | near Karon Circle | tel. 076 37 08 88 | www.ramadaphuketsouthsea. com | Expensive*

KATA NOI BEACH

■ MAP ON PAGE 41
(116 A–B5) (𝄢 C13) **The small *(noi)* Kata Beach is beyond the hill, approx. 15 minutes' walk from the big *(yai)* Kata Beach.**

This bay 1 km/0.5 miles long, with a sandy beach as white as new-fallen snow, is that little bit more beautiful than its larger neighbour, and is also quieter. Kata Noi is like a natural Roman amphitheatre that opens to the sea, flanked by green hills. The elongated Kata Thani Resort dominates the beach but does not rise above the palms and casuarinas, nor block access to the beach. Otherwise there are only a few small hotels, basic restaurants and a handful of shops here.

Beneath the trees: view from Marina Phuket Resort to Karon Beach

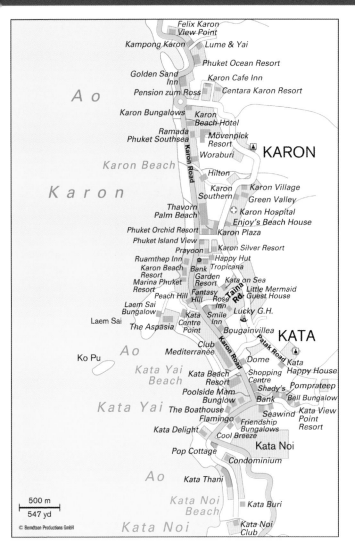

Felix Karon
View Point
Kampong Karon   Lume & Yai
Phuket Ocean Resort
Golden Sand   Karon Cafe Inn
Inn
Pension zum Ross   Centara Karon Resort
A o
Karon Bungalows   Karon
Beach Hotel
Ramada   Mövenpick
Phuket Southsea   Resort
Woraburi   **KARON**
Karon Beach   Hilton
K a r o n   Karon   Karon Village
Southern   Green Valley
Thavorn   Karon Hospital
Palm Beach   Enjoy's Beach House
Phuket Orchid Resort   Karon Plaza
Phuket Island View
Prayoon   Karon Silver Resort
Ruamthep Inn   Happy Hut
Karon Beach   Tropicana
Resort   Bank   Kata on Sea
Marina Phuket   Garden   Little Mermaid
Resort   Resort   Guest House
Fantasy   Rose
Peach Hill   Hill   Inn
Laem Sai   Lucky G.H.
Bungalow   Kata   Smile
Laem Sai   Centre   Inn
The Aspasia   Point   Bougainvillea   **KATA**
A o   Club
Ko Pu   Mediterranée   Dome   Kata
Kata Yai   Shopping   Happy House
Beach   Kata Beach   Centre
Resort   Shady's   Pomprateep
Poolside Mam   Bank   Bell Bungalow
Bunglow   Seawind   Kata View
Kata Yai   The Boathouse   Point
Flamingo   Friendship   Resort
Kata Delight   Bungalows
Cool Breeze
Pop Cottage   **Kata Noi**
Condominium
A o   Kata Thani
Kata Noi   Kata Buri
Beach
500 m   Kata Noi
547 yd   Club
Kata Noi
© Berndtson Productions GmbH

WHERE TO STAY

KATA THANI HOTEL & BEACH RESORT ☺

Tastefully furnished rooms, five restaurants (with European and even Brazilian food), five pools, tennis courts, a gym as well as a sauna – the Kata Thani leaves no wish unfulfilled. It is also environmentally friendly: wastewater is recycled to keep the gardens green, organic fertilisers are used, kitchen leftovers are con-

Kata Noi: a little bay flanked by mountains and with a sandy beach as white as snow

verted to biogas and some of the hot water is heated by solar cells. *480 rooms | 14 Kata Noi Rd. | tel. 076 33 01 24 | www.katathani.com | Expensive*

WHERE TO GO

VIEWPOINT ★ 🎿 (116 B5) (*M C13*)
If you drive from Kata Noi back towards Kata and turn right onto road no. 4233 (towards Nai Harn) directly behind the hill, after 2 km/1.25 miles you reach the *viewpoint* at Kata. High above the sea, it commands a wide-ranging view of the two Kata beaches and of Karon Beach, with beautiful, radiant white crescents of sand lined up like pearls on a chain. The official name for this spot is *Karon Viewpoint*, as it is in the territory of Karon district, to which Kata and Kata Noi belong. There are places to park on the road, and a few stands sell snacks, drinks and souvenirs. A covered pavilion provides shade.

KATA YAI BEACH

MAP ON PAGE 41
(116 B4–5) (*M C12–13*) **A crescent-shaped bay 2 km/1.25 miles long with a superb beach and pure, clear water.**
Almost three quarters of the bay has been occupied by the Club Med, but via the beach road in front of the club you can reach the sea everywhere. Two holiday villages, one at each end of the beach, supply everything tourists need. From the northern village, however, it takes almost ten minutes to get to either Karon beach on the right or to Kata Yai beach on the left. This is a very crowded place, which means there is plenty of atmosphere, but you cannot have a peaceful stroll, as traffic is heavy in the main season. There are many smaller

resorts and guesthouses here, and therefore fewer people on package holidays than on Karon Beach. If you prefer things not to be too quiet, but don't like a place with big hotels, Kata Beach is the right destination.

FOOD & DRINK

THE BOATHOUSE WINE & GRILL

Elegant but casual, with a terrace right on the beach. Both the Thai meals and the international dishes are first class, and the wine list offers an excellent selection. *Daily 7am–11.30pm | in the Boathouse resort | 182 Khok Tanot Rd. | tel. 076 33 05 57 | Expensive*

EUROS DELI

Jo Jo, who has been a chef in various places around the world, cooks up such treats as crabmeat ravioli with mango sauce and smoked duck breast with sweet potatoes and white raisin sauce. The restaurant is three minutes from the centre of Kata (opposite the crazy golf). *Daily | 58–60 Karon Rd. | tel. 076 28 62 65 | Moderate*

INSIDER TIP KAMPONG KATA HILL

This romantic Thai restaurant built from wood lies high on a hill in the middle of Kata. Steaks are served, but fish with chilli sauce is a better option here. *Daily dinner | Kata Centre | Taina Rd. | tel. 076 33 01 03 | Moderate*

MOM TRI'S KITCHEN ★ ☼

An unusual eatery high above the sea on a promontory between Kata and Kata Noi. A fusion of Asian and Mediterranean cooking is the order of the day. Attached to a high-class resort, the restaurant is adorned with works of art and a culinary highlight. Booking recommended. *Mom Tri's Villa Royale | daily lunch/dinner | 3/2 Patak Rd. | tel. 076 33 35 68 | www.momtriphuket.com | Expensive*

RE KATA BEACHCLUB ●

An extremely pleasant place where you can relax on the beach until late at night, with a pool, spa and loungers, light meals, cocktails and many kinds of coffee. The 1000 baht admission charge is deducted from the cost of food and drink. *Daily 9am–midnight | Koktanode Rd. (near the Boathouse resort) | tel. 076 33 04 42 | www.rekataphuket.com | Expensive*

SHOPPING

Kata Beach is not a shopping destination, but you will find everything for your daily needs here and of course all kinds of souvenirs. Nice pottery is for sale at *Earth to Art (Karon Rd. | opposite Dino Park),* and fashionable beachwear next door at INSIDER TIP *Barü (www.barufashion.com).*

SPORTS & ACTIVITIES

A variety of water sports are on offer on the beach. A reef marked by buoys at the north end of the bay is suitable for snorkelling. When the waves are high and roll in at regular intervals (especially at the beginning and end of the rainy season), Kata's surfers get on their boards. At *Phuket Surf* you can hire a board and also take surfing lessons *(www.phuketsurf.com).*

ENTERTAINMENT

The nightlife revolves around bars serving beer on the road from the *Kata Centre* towards Kata Noi. *Easy Riders* is a pub with live music on Taina Road opposite the 7-Eleven shop, where it usually gets lively from about 10pm. Bob Marley would have felt at home in the atmospheric INSIDER TIP *Ska Bar* at the south end of the beach (near the Boathouse resort). The perfect spot for a sundowner and live jazz is *Ratri Jazztaurant (Kata Hill Rd. | www.ratrijazztaurant.com)* high above the sea on Kata Hill.

WHERE TO STAY

THE ASPASIA ☆

This resort with classy design lies high up with fantastic views and spoils its guests with every imaginable luxury. The size of the rooms and suites is between 65 and 210 m² (700–2300 sq ft). Spa, two pools. Steep steps take you down to the beach in only two minutes. *84 rooms | 1/3 Laem Sai Rd. | tel. 076 33 30 33 | www.aspasia phuket.com | Expensive*

KATA BEACH SPA RESORT

The name is misleading, as there is no longer a spa here. The ten cottages are fairly basic, but all have air-conditioning, TV and refrigerator, and are situated in green surroundings on a hill between the Kata Centre and the beach. You will hardly find a more reasonably priced bungalow at Kata Beach. *95 Pakbang Rd. | tel. 076 33 09 14 | www.katabeach sparesort.com | Budget–Moderate*

INSIDER TIP KATA DELIGHT VILLAS

An intimate oasis of peace and quiet beneath palms and mature deciduous trees. Comfortable bungalows with sea view on the Kata side of the hill between Kata Yai and Kata Noi (turn off after the Boathouse resort). *16 rooms | 186/15 Khok Tanot | tel. 076 33 06 36 | www.katade light.com | Expensive*

KATA GARDEN RESORT

Clean bungalows and rooms in a hotel with air-conditioning and minibar in a well-tended garden with pool on the hill between Kata and Karon. The walk to the beaches takes just under ten minutes. *65 rooms | 32 Karon Rd. | tel. 076 33 06 27 | www.katagar denphuket.com | Moderate–Expensive*

THE LITTLE MERMAID

Simple, clean rooms with air-conditioning, some of them with TV and minibar, in the guesthouse or in bungalows around a small pool. Good value for money. The beaches of Karon and Kata are both approx. 15 minutes away on foot. *40 rooms | Patak Rd. | near junction with Taina Rd. | tel. 076 33 07 30 | www.littlemermaid phuket.net | Budget–Moderate*

LAYAN BEACH

(112 A6) *(ⓜ C6)* **On the hills inland from this beach between Nai Thon and Bang Tao many luxury apartments and holiday homes have been built.**
Phuket's ultimate exclusive resort hides away on the wooded *Cape Laem Son* in Layan district.

WHERE TO STAY

TRISARA ★

Luxury resort above a small nameless beach of fine-grained sand (stony at low water) with 39 villas, generously spaced across 70,000 m²/17 acres of green hilly country. Lots of wood and marble, and each house has a pool and sea view. From approx. 690 euros per night. *60/1 Moo 6 | Srisoonthorn Rd. | Choeng Thale | tel. 076 31 01 00 | www.trisara.com | Expensive*

MAI KHAO BEACH

(112 A–B3) *(ⓜ C3)* **Phuket's longest beach (10 km/6 miles) in the north was**

the last to be developed for tourism.
The few resorts are still spaced well apart here, and there is no danger of this beach being completely built up, as much of the terrain is part of the Sirinat National Park. With one exception the resorts on Mai Khao are all in the top category. There are neither loungers nor pubs nor souvenir shops on this beach. It is perfect for those who like long, lonely walks along the sand.

SIGHTSEEING

SIRINAT NATIONAL PARK ● ☺
(112 A1) (*∅ C1–2*)
At the north end of the beach near the visitor centre of Sirinat National Park, access has been created to the INSIDERTIP *mangrove jungle*. You can take a look at this tidal biotope from raised walkways. With a little luck you might spot a monitor lizard. The entrance to the visitor centre lies on the old road to the mainland (on the right) approx. 1 km/half a mile before you reach Sarasin Bridge, which is no longer open to traffic. *Daily 8.30am–4.30pm | admission 200 baht | www.dnp. go.th (for all national parks)*

FOOD & DRINK

There are no independent places to eat and drink on the beach near the resorts, but in the little *Turtle Village* shopping centre next to the Anantara Resort you can get ice cream at *Swensens*, beer at the *Bill Bentley Pub*, western and Thai dishes at the *Coffee Club* and food from a supermarket.

SHOPPING

You will find several high-class boutiques in *Turtle Village (www.royalgardenplaza. co.th/turtlevillage)*

WHERE TO STAY

INSIDERTIP MAI KHAO BEACH BUNGALOW
The lowest-priced resort on the whole beach by a long way. The bungalows are simply furnished but clean and have air-conditioning or a fan. The restaurant serves good Thai food, and you can have a massage beneath a canopy of palm fronds. *6 rooms | Mai Khao (near the Holiday Inn) | tel. 0818 95 12 33 | www. maikhaobeach.wordpress.com | Budget–Moderate*

MARRIOT'S MAI KHAO BEACH ☺
One of Phuket's top resorts, with superb restaurants, a gym, tennis courts, three pools and the island's biggest ● health and beauty spa. The resort makes an effort to protect the turtles that lay their eggs on Mai Khao between November and February. *265 rooms | Mai Khao | tel. 076 33 80 00 | www.marriott.com | Expensive*

A sea of flowers: a fragrant bath in the spa of the Marriott Phuket luxury resort

Everything is the finest quality in this luxury resort between the beach and an artificial lake. It goes without saying that there is a pool, spa and gym, as well as yoga courses on the beach. Three restaurants, a café, a pub. In the Kids Club younger guests can run around under the supervision of trained staff or devote themselves to Playstations when their parents feel like having a quiet time. *180 rooms | Mai Khao | tel. 076 36 39 99 | www.renaissancephuket.com | Expensive*

This resort is very trendy and characterised by simple elegance. Luxurious houses, three pools and spa. *79 rooms | Mai Khao | tel. 076 33 88 88 | www.salaphuket.com | Expensive*

LOW BUDGET

▶ The basic Karon Bungalows only cost 500 baht. Shower and fan, only 100 m/100 yd to the beach. *17 rooms | Karon Beach | 236 Karon Rd. (by the roundabout) | tel. 0893 90 40 97*

▶ With air-conditioning and TV from 1000 baht, with a fan from 600 baht. Centrally located in Kata, but quiet and only ten minutes from the beach. *Fantasy Hill Bungalow | 34 rooms | Kata Beach | 8/1 Karon Rd. | tel. 076 33 01 06 | www.sites. google.com/site/fantasyhillbungalow*

▶ You can find a hearty meal for only a few baht on Patong Beach at the stalls along the narrow dead-end road that branches off from Soi Bangla at the Family Pharmacy.

NAI THON BEACH

(112 A5) (*ⓜ B–C5*) **Water buffalo still pasture behind the beach of fine-grained sand, but Nai Thon is slowly awakening from its slumber.**

A few resorts and one large hotel have now sprung up along the beach road, and several restaurants and shops have appeared for the benefit of holidaymakers, but Nai Thon is still one of the quietest beaches on Phuket, and few day trippers come here, as it is some distance away from the main tourist centres.

FOOD & DRINK

A few beach pubs serve simple meals and drinks. For good Thai meals, head for *Wiwan's* on the beach road.

WHERE TO STAY

None of the resorts are situated directly on the beach, so wherever you are staying, you cross a quiet road to get down to the sea.

THE ANGEL OF NAITHON

A cosy complex with rustic charm. Comfortable wooden bungalows plus rooms in a building around the pool. Even if you do not stay here, it is worth looking in to see the veteran Volkswagen Beetles. The owner, Mr Miyos, collects them and is happy to stop for a chat. *10 rooms | Nai Thon Beach | tel. 08 18 30 96 28 | www. angelofnaithon.com | Moderate–Expensive*

NAITHON BEACH RESORT

Spacious rooms with varied fittings. For budget travellers there are rooms with a

Dense jungle covers the hills behind the beaches of Nai Thon and Nai Yang

fan for about 25 euros. Spa with sauna. *45 rooms | Nai Thon Beach | tel. 076 20 52 33 | www.phuketnaithonresort. com | Moderate–Expensive*

NAITHONBURI BEACH RESORT
This three-storey building around a pool is the best accommodation on Nai Thon Beach by a mile. *232 rooms | Nai Thon Beach | tel. 076 31 87 00 | www.naithon buri.com | Expensive*

WHERE TO GO

INSIDER TIP ▶ **HIN KRUAI** ●
(114 A1) (∅ B6)
The name of this little bay means 'banana rock' – and so the beach has to be Banana Beach. A little paradise, not built up, with snow-white sand and a blue sea. You can get snacks and drinks in a beach bar, but it is perfectly possible, even in the high season, that only you and a few others leave footprints in the sand here. On many maps the bay is not even marked and it is easy to overlook, as you cannot see it from the road. When you

drive towards Patong from Nai Thon Beach, after approx. 1 km/half a mile look out for a weathered sign (Banana Beach) by the roadside. An unpaved path leads down to the beach through dense vegetation.

NAI YANG BEACH

(112 A4) (∅ C4) **Woods of long-needled casuarinas extend between the sea and rubber plantations. In the jungle-covered hills further inland, wild boar roam through the undergrowth.**
This beach is ideal for families and nature lovers. Close to the airport, Nai Yang Beach, which is 2 km/1.25 miles long, merges with the 10 km/6-mile-long Mai Khao Beach. Accommodation directly on the beach is available only in a few resorts and in the spartan bungalows managed by the national park.
The few options for staying in Nai Yang are several minutes' walk from the beach.

Offshore coral reefs forming a natural breakwater, and the shallow waters of Nai Yang Beach ensure that swimming is not dangerous even in the monsoon season, as it is on many other beaches.

SIGHTSEEING

NATIONAL PARK ☺

The whole of Nai Yang Beach is officially part of Sirinat National Park, which is marked as the Nai Yang National Park on many maps. The northern part of the beach has not been built up. The small museum run by the national park authority informs visitors about the fauna of the area, with exhibitions of shells, corals and insects. *Daily 8.30am–noon and 1pm–4.30pm | the museum is free, but foreigners have to pay a 200-baht admission charge to enter the park. It costs 30 baht extra to drive through in your car.*

FOOD & DRINK

Many food stalls and open-air restaurants. The shade provided by the trees makes Nai Yang a popular picnic spot for the Thais.

INSIDER TIP ▶ RIVET GRILL

Those in the know make the journey from the far south of the island up here to the north for Sunday brunch in this restaurant, which belongs to the *Indigo Pearl*. Sushi, steaks, pasta, oysters, bread, cheese and cake, with unlimited wine thrown in, costs 2150 baht. The *Kids Club* of the resort looks after children, who can eat for free if they are under 12 years old. *Daily dinner, brunch Sun noon–1pm (booking recommended) | tel. 076 32 70 06 | Moderate–Expensive*

SPORTS & ACTIVITIES

PHUKET KITE SCHOOL

Surfing powered by the wind: from May until the end of October you can learn how to zoom across the waves, pulled by a steerable kite. A one-hour beginner's course costs 1200 baht. *Beach Rd. | tel. 08 00 77 75 94 | www.kiteschool phuket.com*

For the rest of the year, the school moves across to the bay of Chalong *(Wiset Rd.)*, because the wind is better there in this period.

WHERE TO STAY

DANG SEA BEACH BUNGALOW

These bungalows are located beneath casuarina trees in the middle of the beach. Basic but well-kept, with air-conditioning, TV, refrigerator. Plenty of little beach cafés nearby. *10 rooms | Nai Yang Beach | tel. 076 32 83 62 | www.dangsea beach.com | Moderate*

THE GOLDDIGGER'S RESORT

Cosy and well-tended Swiss-run complex. Rooms with TV, refrigerator, air-conditioning or fan in terraced houses around the pool. 50 m/50 yd to the beach. *26 rooms | 74/12 Surin Rd. | tel. 0 76 32 84 24 | www.golddigger-resortcom | Budget–Moderate*

INDIGO PEARL

This top-quality resort was refurbished in summer 2012. Spa, three pools, two tennis courts, four restaurants. Those who like it really romantic can dine right on the beach in the evenings. Courses in yoga, Pilates and even Thai kick-boxing. *290 rooms | Nai Yang Beach | tel. 076 32 70 06 | www.indigo-pearl.com | Expensive*

PANSEA BEACH

(114 A3) *(M B7–8)* **This small bay is separated from Bang Tao by a wooded rocky headland and sheltered by the slopes of a hill right behind the beach.** Pansea Beach is a world of its own. Which is appreciated by guests at two luxury resorts, *Amanpuri* and *The Surin*, situated high above the sea.

FOOD & DRINK

The restaurants of the high-class resorts on Pansea Beach are excellent – but unfortunately fairly expensive. The beach bars and eateries on *Surin Beach* are cheaper, and it takes only ten minutes to walk there.

WHERE TO STAY

AMANPURI
Beautifully fitted bungalows in classic Thai style. Even though it is no longer brand new, Amanpuri is still right up there in the world league of top resorts, as the presence of sports stars and celebrities such as Robert de Niro confirms. You will not be disappointed, providing you are able to pay 800 euros per night for the pleasure. *40 rooms | 118 Srisoonthorn Rd. | tel. 076 32 43 33 | www. amanresorts.com | Expensive*

THE SURIN
What was once called Chedi has now been renamed and completely refurbished, with the work completed in summer 2012. Shingle-roofed luxury bungalows in grey-and-white retro design built on a slope. The clientele is not quite so elite as in the

World-class: international stars take holidays at the Amanpuri Beach resort

Amanpuri next door, but then The Surin is significantly cheaper (from approx. 300 euros). The black-tiled octagonal pool is a real eye-catcher. *103 rooms | 118 Srisoonthorn Rd. | tel. 076 62 15 80 | www.thesurinphuket.com | Expensive*

PATONG BEACH

MAP ON PAGE 51
(116 A–B2) (*ω C10*) In the 1970s globetrotters stayed here in bamboo huts. Now hotels occupy the site, and a town is spreading where boys herded water buffalo as late as the 1980s.
Patong has turned into what many tourists want to see: a great big noisy place of entertainment. Whether you are looking for a bar, a boutique or your favourite meals from back home – here you will find all of these things. On the 3 km/2-mile-long beach, deck chairs and loungers are crowded together in rows.
In the centre of this tourist town, masses of visitors throng the stores and tailors' shops. Loud music emanates from hundreds of bars, and an army of girls, boys and *ladyboys* (transvestites and transsexuals) lie in wait for men to spend the night with – or the rest of their life. Patong Beach is no finishing school for posh girls, but a place where sailors come looking for some fun. Indeed, ships of the US Navy sometimes anchor in the bay. You will not find any of Phuket's top-class resort hotels here, but slowly things are changing. The first carefully designed clubs are adding a bit of quality to the nightlife, and some chic restaurants and a few stylish boutique resorts have opened here. *www.patong-beach.com*

FOOD & DRINK

There is an enormous choice here. International or Thai food, low-cost or exclusive – Patong Beach has something for every taste. The food prepared on street stalls is the best value for money, and often the tastiest you will get. Many INSIDER TIP mobile cooks can be found from late afternoon along the wall of the Muslim cemetery in the middle of the beach.

Shops, stalls, bars and street traders: there is always a lot going on at Patong Beach

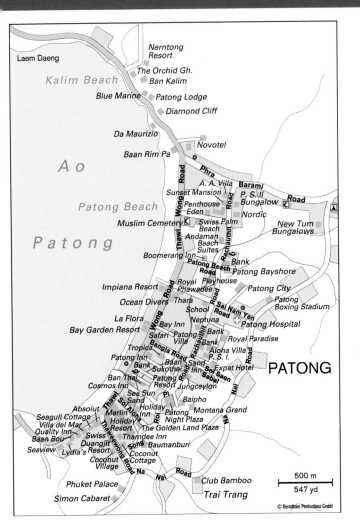

Nerntong Resort
Laem Daeng
The Orchid Gh.
Kalim Beach
Ban Kalim
Blue Marine
Patong Lodge
Diamond Cliff
Da Maurizio
Novotel
Baan Rim Pa
Phra
A o
A. A. Villa
Barami
Sunset Mansion
P. S. II
Bungalow
Patong Beach
Penthouse
Eden
Nordic
Muslim Cemetery
Swiss Palm
Beach
New Tum
Bungalows
P a t o n g
Andaman
Beach
Suites
Boomerang Inn
Patong Beach
Road
Bank
Patong Bayshore
Impiana Resort
Royal
Phawadee
Playhouse
Patong City
Ocean Divers
Thara
School
Patong
Boxing Stadium
La Flora
Road
Neptuna
Patong Hospital
Bay Garden Resort
Bay Inn
Safari
Patong
Villa
Bank
Royal Paradise
Tropica
Bangla Road
Bank
Aloha Villa
Patong Inn
Baan Sand
P. S. I.
Bank
Sukothai
Sol Saen
Expat Hotel
PATONG
Ban Thai
Patong
Sabai
Cosmos Inn
Resort
Jungceylon
Sea Sun
Baipho
Sand
Absolut
Holiday
Patong
Montana Grand
Merlin
Inn
Night Plaza
Seagull Cottage
Holiday
Villa del Mar
Resort
The Golden Land Plaza
Quality Inn
Swiss
Thamdee Inn
Baan Bou
Duangjit
Baumanburi
Seaview
Lydia's Resort
Coconut
Coconut
Cottage
Village
Na
Nai
Road
Phuket Palace
Club Bamboo
Simon Cabaret
Trai Trang

Sai Nam Yen
Road

Thawi Wong Road
Rachauthit Road
Sawatdirak Road
Nai Road
Thawewong Road
Song Road

500 m
547 yd

© Berndtson Productions GmbH

BAAN RIM PA ❄

The veteran of Patong's top restaurants, at the north end of town, is still excellent. Piano music forms the accompaniment to royal Thai cuisine, which means that the ingredients are as fresh as can be and that the dishes are presented with artistic flair – a treat for the eyes and the palate. *Daily lunch/dinner | 223 Kalim Beach Rd. | tel. 076 34 07 89 | www.baan rimpa.com | Moderate–Expensive*

JOE'S DOWNSTAIRS

As the name says, you go down steps from the street, and enter a joint just above the water where everything is white. This is a lovely place to sip a sundowner. The food is New World cuisine, ranging from a Portobello burger to rock lobster with mango. *Daily lunch/dinner | 223/3 Kalim Beach Rd. | next to Baan Rim Pa | tel. 076 34 42 54 | www.joesphuket. com | Expensive*

THE 9TH FLOOR

Swiss sausage salad and steaks, Thai prawn soup and risotto. Normally this kind of crazy mixture sets off the alarm bells, but here the quality is truly good, and the view from the ⚞ open-air restaurant on the ninth floor is a winner. *Daily from 4pm | 47 Rat Uthit Rd. | in the Sky Inn Condotel | tel. 076 34 43 11 | www. the9thfloor.com | Moderate–Expensive*

INSIDER TIP PUM RESTAURANT

Classic, down-to-earth Thai cooking such as fried noodles and curry is on the menu here. You can watch the cooks at work in this open restaurant. And in ● *Pum's Cooking School* you can put on the chef's apron yourself. *Daily until 9pm | 204/32 Rat Uthit Rd. | next to Christine Massage | tel. 076 34 62 69 | www.pumthaifood chain.com | Budget*

SALA BUA

Out-of-the-ordinary creations such as duck ravioli as well as classic Thai dishes such as green curry with chicken area served in this eatery. Diners enjoy this delicious food right on the beach in the *Impiana* resort. *Daily from 12 noon | 41 Taweewong Rd. | tel. 076 34 01 38 | www. sala-bua.com | Expensive*

BOOKS & FILMS

▶ **The Lioness in Bloom** – A collection of short stories about Thai women, some of them written by women.

▶ **Travelers' Tales: Thailand** – A lively and revealing collection of stories and reports by different authors, including Pico Iyer and Norman Lewis.

▶ **The Man with the Golden Gun** – James Bond film with Roger Moore and Christopher Lee (1974). Director Guy Hamilton filmed spectacular scenes in the bay of Phang Nga – since then one of the islands has been named after Bond.

▶ **Phra Farang** – The experiences of Peter Robinson, who spent ten years as a monk (phra) in a monastery. His book provides insights into a world that is

normally not accessible to outsiders.

▶ **King Bhumibol Adulyadej** – An interesting biography of the world's longest-reigning monarch by Nicholas Grossman.

▶ **Cutthroat Island** – This confused story of a treasure hunter directed by Renny Harlin with his wife Geena Davis as a female pirate (1995) was a major box-office flop, but the scenery is magnificent. The movie was filmed around the cliffs of Phang Nga and Krabi.

▶ **The Beach** – A story about searching for paradise, directed by Danny Boyle and starring Leonardo DiCaprio (2000). The locations include Ko Phi Phi and Phuket – footage that›ll make you want to book a flight.

Not only the view is heart-stopping: bungee jumping from a 50 metre/165-ft tower

SHOPPING

Shops, stalls, countless street traders – and in spite of all of this, it is difficult to find anything original, as the offerings consist of souvenir tat and copied products. The biggest shopping centre, with a department store, smaller shops and restaurants, is ● *Jungceylon (www.jung ceylon.com)* on *Ra Uthit Rd.*

SPORTS & ACTIVITIES

Parasailing, windsurfing on the beach, water-skiing; diving expeditions and courses can be booked at many diving stations. You can ride on an elephant in *Camp Chang Kalim (daily 8.30am– 6.30pm | www.campchang.com)* on Kalim Beach just to the north of Patong Beach. Roar around the track at the *Go Kart Speedway (daily 10am–10pm | tel. 076 32 19 49 | www.gokartthailand.com)*

on the road towards Phuket Town. A few miles further on, turn off left to *Kathu Waterfall,* and shortly before it to a lake where *Phuket Waterski Cableways (tel. 076 20 25 25 | daily 9am–9pm)* tows water-skiers (including children from the age of five) over the water at 28 kmh/18 mph. Elephant rides and a monkey-and-elephant show *(11am and 4pm)* are also on the programme.

If you have always wanted to jump off a tower from a height of 50m/165ft, then don't miss the *Jungle Bungy Jump (tel. 076 32 13 51 | www.phuketbungy.com)* on a small lake halfway to Phuket Town (signposted). If you prefer a quiet life, on the top floor of *Ocean Plaza (Soi Bangla)* and at *Strike Bowl* in the Jungceylon shopping centre you can go bowling from midday to midnight. For jogging with a group and a party afterwards, join the hard-drinking *Hash House Harriers (www.phuket-hhh.com)*, who run a different route every Saturday. There are gym facilities outside the major hotels *(www. phuket.com/sports/fitness.htm)*.

ENTERTAINMENT

Beer bars on every corner and go-go bars in the centre of Patong do brisk business. The epicentre of nightlife is around ● *Soi Bangla* and its side streets. The discos *Crocodile* and *Dragon* can be found in this entertainment district. The dance club with the best light-and-sound system there is *Seduction (www.seductiondisco. com)*. *Banana Disco* at the *Patong Beach Hotel* is popular amongst the expatriates who live on Phuket, and Japanese tourists.

In Soi Bangla pimped-up *ladyboys* tout for customers every evening for the transvestite show in the *Moulin Rose*. In return for a tip they are happy to pose in front of tourists' cameras. The show itself *(several times daily from 9.30pm)* is okay, but it can't compete with the splendid costumes in the ★ *Simon Cabaret (daily 7.30 and 9.30pm | www.phuket-simon cabaret.com)* on the road to Karon. In a fast-paced performance with music, dancing and comedy up to 50 'ladies' take to the stage for a show lasting a bit over an hour.

In the *Hard Rock Cafe* by the Marriott Hotel a live band plays daily from 10pm. The café also has a shop with souvenirs for fans of rock music. A touch of Las Vegas has also been in the air on Patong Beach since 2011: dancing and comedy, acrobatics and magic constitute the entertainment at the *Danze Fantasy Theatre*

A blaze of colour: the transvestite show at Simon Cabaret

(Tue–Sun from 9pm | www.danzefantasy. com) on Soi Bangla. A few paces further along, loud, hard rock is on offer at the *Rock Star* on Soi Bangla as well as in *Rock City*, at the junction of Soi Bangla and Rat-U-Thit Rd. The sound next door in the *Tai Pan* club *(www.taipan.st)* is loud and heavy. The hippest club on the scene is INSIDER TIP *Sound (www.soundphuket. com)* in Jungceylon, the island's biggest shrine to the cult of shopping. With its clever light effects and architecture without any corners (it is modelled on the human ear), it might be a set for a science-fiction film.

Blows are traded with hands and feet in the *Patong Boxing Stadium (every Mon and Thu from 9pm)*. The best places for people-watching on Soi Bangla are the *Kangaroo Bar*, which is almost as old as Patong itself (and looks that way too), and the pubs for hardcore drinkers to the left and right of it.

WHERE TO STAY

Not many hotels are situated right on the beach. Please bear in mind that it is not acceptable in Thailand to walk to the beach wearing swimming shorts or a bikini.

INSIDER TIP BAIPHO

This little gem of a boutique hotel lies hidden in a side street leading to the *Montana Grand* hotel. Swiss fashion photographer Rudi Horber has styled it from top to bottom, from the indirect lighting to the works of art on the walls. Air-conditioning, minibar, DVD players, and use of the Montana Grand's pool. Ten minutes to the beach. *19 rooms | 205/12–13 Rat Uthit Rd. | tel. 076 29 20 74 | www. baipho.com | Moderate*

BOOMERANG INN

Plain, clean rooms in this three-storey guesthouse with a small pool are equipped with TV, minibar and air-conditioning. Central location, five minutes from the beach. *61 rooms | 5/1–8 Hat Patong Rd. (Patong Beach Rd.) | tel. 076 34 21 82 | www.boomeranginn.com | Budget–Moderate*

DUANGJITT RESORT

Hotel and bungalow complex in a large park. Three pools, spa. At the quieter south end of Patong Beach. Three minutes to the beach. *508 rooms | 18 Phachanukhork Rd. | tel. 076 34 07 78 | www.duangjittresort-spa.com | Expensive*

ORCHID RESIDENCE

Cosy guesthouse with air-conditioning, TV, DVD players, refrigerators in the rooms. Seven minutes from the beach. *16 rooms | 171 Soi Sansabai | tel. 076 34 51 76 | www.orchid-residence.com | Budget-Moderate*

ROYAL PHAWADEE VILLAGE

A tropical garden with trees surrounds this charming resort. Wooden houses in the style of north Thailand with balcony, air-conditioning, TV. Pool beneath palms, five minutes to the beach. *36 rooms | 3 Sawatdirak Rd. | tel. 076 34 46 22 | www. royal-phawadee-village.com | Expensive*

TROPICA

You only have to cross the road to get to the beach, and the bar district is round the corner – this resort has a very central location, but with its lushly planted garden nevertheless forms a green oasis in the middle of all the action. Rooms in a two-storey building or bungalows clustering around a pool. All rooms with air-conditioning, refrigerator and TV. *86 rooms | 132 Thaweewong Rd. at the cor-*

ner of Soi Bangla | tel. 076 34 02 04 | www.tropica-bungalow.de | Expensive

WHERE TO GO

FREEDOM BEACH (116 A3) (*ill B11*)
At the south end of Patong Beach longtails set off from a floating pier to take day trippers an a 30-minute voyage around a headland to picturesque Freedom Beach *(return journey approx. 1200 baht incl. waiting time)*. There are no hotels there, only a basic restaurant. The loungers on this beach of fine-grained sand are usually all taken, but compared to Patong, Freedom Beach is quiet and relaxing. The water is clear enough for snorkelling. On the way there you pass *Paradise Beach*, also known as *Diamond Beach*, which is quieter but equally beautiful.

SURIN BEACH

(114 A3) (*ill C8*) **Surin Beach, about 500 metres long, has been transformed from a place for water buffalo into a luxury beach.**
The hills behind Surin Beach are gradually being built up with fine homes. On the main road classy boutiques in *Plaza* cater for wealthy customers. But low-cost accommodation can still be found, as well as peace and quiet.

FOOD & DRINK

Most of the simpler beach bars have made way for higher-class restaurants. The trendiest of them, with ingenious indirect lighting of the bar, is the *Catch Beach Club (www.catchbeachclub.com | Expensive)* belonging to the luxury resort *Twin Palms*. Enjoy their excellent beach barbecue with live music for 1190 baht every Tuesday and Friday *(tel. 076*

31 65 67 for bookings). In the beach restaurant **INSIDER TIP** *Taste (www.tastesurinbeach.com | Expensive)* the tuna carpaccio and warm goat's cheese salad with balsamico dressing melt in your mouth.

INSIDER TIP CUDOS
This restaurant with simple but elegant design opened in 2011 and specialises in Mediterranean cuisine. You can follow up the saffron risotto with a creme brulée, and of course there are wines to match the dishes. The open-air zone is designed like a small theatre. On Saturday evenings bands play live music, or cinema classics such as Casablanca are screened. *Mon–Sat from 5pm | on the main road near the Plaza shopping centre | tel. 076 38 65 98 | www.cudosrestaurant.com | Expensive*

OPUS ONE
How about beef carpaccio followed by truffle risotto? The Mediterranean-influenced menu in this top-quality restaurant approx. 5 minutes from the beach is small but classy, and the list of fine wines is all the more extensive. Enjoy your meal either in the air-conditioned restaurant or outdoors on the roof of the exclusive The Plaza Surin shopping mall. *Daily dinner | on the main road towards Bang Thao | tel. 076 38 65 62 | www.opusone phuket.com | Expensive*

SHOPPING

The Plaza Surin on the main road is an upmarket shopping centre where the owners of villas in this area come to look for furniture, art and antiques. *Soul of Asia*, one of the island's best antique shops, is based here. Clothes and a better quality of souvenirs are also sold here. A short distance away you can buy Euro-

Beautiful and popular: Laem Singh Bay

pean wines from the *Central Wine Cellar*. On the beach road next to the Surin Bay Inn, *Lemongrass* is filled with the scents of soap, lotions, bath salts and other home-made spa products.

WHERE TO STAY

BENYADA LODGE
Elegant boutique hotel with simple design. Rooms have air-conditioning, TV and minibar. Roof terrace with bar and loungers for sunbathing. Only two minutes to the beach. *29 rooms | Surin Beach | tel. 076 27 12 61 | www.benyada lodge-phuket.com | Expensive*

SURIN BAY INN
Small and cosy, only three minutes' walk from the beach. When you stand on the balcony of your room, the view extends to the whole bay. Well-kept rooms with air-conditioning, TV, refrigerator, and excellent value for money by the standards of expensive Surin Beach. *12 rooms | Surin Beach | tel. 076 27 16 01 | www. surinbayinn.com | Moderate*

SURIN SWEET HOTEL
Large, clean rooms with air-conditioning, balcony, refrigerator, TV. Pool. *30 rooms | Surin Beach | tel. 076 27 08 63 | Moderate*

TWIN PALMS
Top resort, to design from top to bottom. Luxurious rooms, some with their own pool. *76 rooms | Surin Beach | tel. 076 31 65 00 | www.twinpalms-phuket.com | Expensive*

WHERE TO GO

LAEM SINGH ☀️ (114 A3) (ᗰ (C8)
At the Lion Cape, 1.5 km/1 mile south of Surin on the road towards Patong Beach, what may be the most scenically beautiful bay on Phuket is situated below the road: rocks as on the Seychelles, and a little stream that flows from the foot of the green hills across the fine sand of the beach into the sea. As it is near to Patong Beach, a lot of motorboats come here, and the beach is always busy. There are no hotels, but several beach restaurants. Parking spaces are available up on the road.

SOUTH AND EAST COAST

Although the capital of Phuket lies on the east coast, outside the town little has been changed by tourism. Which is why the east coast is a popular residential area for expatriates who live on Phuket.

Most of the beaches are muddy and stony. Mangrove swamps and farms for prawns and crabs line the coast. To the south of the harbour of Phuket however, beyond Cape Phan Wa, and in the bay of Chalong, adventurous holidaymakers will find acceptable beaches. Above all, the area inland from here remains largely authentic. And in the far south there are even two picturesque bays and a fantastic beach.

AO CHALONG

(116–117 C–D 4–5) (𝐷 E–F12) **The bay of Chalong is a popular point of anchorage for sailing yachts from all over the world, which find shelter from the monsoon storms here.**

Fisherman land their catch, and in the backcountry goats graze in plantations of coconut palms. Only a few miles south of the pier, *Mittrapab (Friendship) Beach* and *Laem Ka Beach are clean*, but swimming is only possible at high tide. Roads lead down to the water and to the few places to stay. It is also possible to take a boat out to the offshore islands. If you are looking for peace and quiet and have a car or moped, you will be content here.

Photo: Nai Harn Beach

Few tourists – more authentic,
with everyday village life and
stunning sunsets

SIGHTSEEING

BIG BUDDHA ⭐

While the whole site has not yet been completed, with a height of 45 m/150 ft, the enormous Buddha at an altitude of 400 m/1300 ft on Nagakerd Mountain is already an overwhelming sight. Financed entirely by donations, it will probably take a few more years to bring construction of the complex to an end. However, the figure is already highly impressive, and the views are fantastic. *Admission free | near Chalong on the main road towards the airport; turn-off signposted| www.mingmongkolphuket.com*

WAT CHALONG ⭐ ●

3 km/2 miles north of the roundabout in the village of Chalong, on the by-pass road to the airport, the red roofs of the largest Buddhist monastery on Phuket shine in the sun. A big fair is held here at Chinese New Year. *Admission free*

AO SANE BEACH

FOOD & DRINK

SEAFOOD RESTAURANTS IN CHALONG BAY

Kang Eang (daily from 11am | tel. 076 38 12 12 | www.kaneang-pier.com | Moderate–Expensive), situated right by the

Staying on Ao Sane Beach – as romantic as it gets and very rustic

pier, is famous. It is particularly charming in the evening, when the lights are reflected in the water. INSIDER TIP *Palai Seafood (daily from 10am | tel. 076 28 21 74 | Moderate–Expensive)*, on the beach 1 km/half a mile beyond Phuket Zoo, is not much frequented by tourists, but here too you can eat very well. *Jimmy's Lighthouse (daily from 9am | tel. 076 38 17 09 | Budget–Moderate)* to the left of Chalong pier is extremely popular

amongst the yachting crowd, who come here to eat burgers.

SPORTS & ACTIVITIES

On the edge of Chalong, a whole row of leisure facilities have opened on the road towards Kata Beach *(all daily 9am–6pm)*. At *Phuket Shooting Range* you can take aim at targets or clay pigeons. *Paintball* allows its visitors to shoot at each other, resulting in no more harm than getting covered in paint. Elephant riding, monkey shows and snake shows are also on offer.

WHERE TO STAY

FRIENDSHIP BEACH RESORT

This veteran among resorts on Phuket, halfway between Chalong and Rawai, is popular with long-term guests. Rooms, apartments, bungalows with every amenity. Pool by the sea. Fri and Sun jam sessions. *40 rooms | Soi Mittrapab | tel. 076 28 89 96 | www.friendshipbeach. com | Expensive*

SHANTI LODGE

Small, well-run establishment in a quiet side street approx. 1 km/half a mile north of the Chalong roundabout on the bypass road. With a seawater pool and restaurant; choose between air-conditioning or fan. *14 rooms | 1/2 Soi Bangrae | Choafa Nok Rd. | tel. 076 28 02 33 | www. shantilodge.com | Budget*

AO SANE BEACH

(116 A–B6) (*QI C14*) **This** INSIDER TIP **romantic rocky cove lies at the end of the road that leads from Nai Harn Beach**

and passes beneath the yacht club, first up and then down a hill.

This is a little world of its own along two tiny beaches, where corals emerge from the water at low tide. For children these beaches are not suitable, as there is a risk of injury. Everything has remained in a fairly natural condition, and two resorts share this little paradise. A lot of day trippers come here, however, when they find other beaches too crowded for their taste.

SPORTS & ACTIVITIES

The only diving base on Phuket that is right by the beach is run by multilingual Armin and Sylvia at *Ao Sane Bungalows*. You can walk to your diving baptism on the local reef. *www.armins-diveteam.de*

WHERE TO STAY

BAAN KRATING JUNGLE BEACH

Spacious wooden and concrete bungalows with air-conditioning, TV and minibar beneath leafy trees. Small pool. The food is better and cheaper in the restaurant of the neighbouring *Ao Sane Bungalows*. *65 rooms | Ao Sane | tel. 076 28 82 64 | www.baankrating.com | Expensive*

LAEM PHAN WA

(117 E4) (ꬹ F12) **Laem means cape, and the most beautiful beach on the east coast lies on this cape at the foot of green hills, fringed by palms.**

Guests at the resorts have this bay all to themselves. Thanks to a sheltered location, even in the monsoon season there are seldom big waves here. It is a good option for visitors who want a quiet life in comfort and close to town.

SIGHTSEEING

PHUKET AQUARIUM ★ ●

This marine biology base is known as *Phuket Aquarium*. Situated at the southern tip of the cape, it is active in breeding sea turtles in addition to its research activities. All the sea creatures roaming the waters around Phuket, from sharks to the fish living on the coral reefs, can be seen in the aquarium. *Daily 8.30am–4pm | admission 100 baht | Sakdidet Rd. | www.phuketaquarium.org*

FOOD & DRINK

PANWA HOUSE

This enchanting white house looks like the residence of a tin magnate. Thai food is served right on the beach. *Tue–Sun dinner | in the Cape Panwa Hotel | tel. 076 39 11 23 | Moderate–Expensive*

★ **Big Buddha**
Thailand's tallest Buddha on the summit of a hill → p. 59

★ **Wat Chalong**
Phuket's biggest Buddhist temple hosts a fair for Chinese New Year → p. 59

★ **Phuket Aquarium**
Eyeball to eyeball with sharks and coral-reef fish → p. 61

★ **Nai Harn Beach**
A wonderful tropical bay → p. 62

★ **Laem Promthep**
Viewpoint for sunsets → p. 63

MARCO POLO HIGHLIGHTS

WHERE TO STAY

CAPE PANWA HOTEL

Luxurious rooms in the hotel building and six bungalows on the hillside. Pool, tennis courts and even a short cable lift from the hotel down to the beach. *246 rooms | Sakdidet Rd. | Cape Panwa | tel. 076 39 11 23 | www.capepanwa.com | Expensive*

NAI HARN BEACH

(116 B6) *(𝄞 C14)* ★ **Blue sea, a large sandy beach framed by green hill slopes, and a lagoon behind it – no wonder hippies and backpackers were particularly attached to Nai Harn Beach when tourism started up on Phuket.**

The hippies and their huts on stilts have now disappeared, but Nai Harn has not become busy and noisy. Here you will find only two resorts, as well as a few souvenir shops and open-air pubs. Most visitors are day trippers who find the beaches by their own hotels too crowded.

In the high season a lot of sailing yachts anchor here.

FOOD & DRINK

Top-quality food is served in two first-class restaurants in the *Yacht Club (both open daily for dinner | tel. 076 38 11 56 | Moderate–Expensive)*. During happy hour between 6 and 7pm you can sip two sunset cocktails for the price of one on the terrace. Several basic open-air restaurants do business on the approach to the beach and behind the coastal promenade. For delicious cakes and good coffee, try INSIDER TIP ▶ *A Spoonful of Sugar (Tue–Sun 8am–7pm | Budget)*, a charming café with retro design on Saiyuan Rd., opposite the Herbal Sauna. Approx. 300 m/300 yd before you reach it, on the same side of the road, the German Bakery *(daily 7.30am–5.30pm | Budget)* sells freshly baked bread and hearty sausages. Between the café and the bakery, on the left of Saiyuan, *Da Vinci (Mon–Sat for dinner | tel. 076 28 95 74 | www.davinciphuket.com | Moderate–Expensive)* dishes up high-quality Italian food.

AN ALL-PURPOSE TREE

For tourists it symbolises the tropics and the desire to be in a far-away place. But for the Thais, the coconut palm is the ultimate tree. Not only for its large fruit with delicious milk that is as clear as water. The coconut palm is a source of much more. The dried flesh, copra, is made into oil and used for cooking and making soap. The hard inner part of the shell can be used to collect the latex sap from rubber trees,

for example. When dry, the outer part of the shell is fuel for cooking. The straight trunk of palm trees can be sawn into boards. The palm fronds can be woven to make a roof covering that stands up to the heaviest monsoon rain, at least for a few years. And the best characteristic of this all-purpose tree is that it is not demanding, and grows as well on wet pastures as on a hot sandy beach.

Laem Promthep: this rocky cape is a popular vantage point for spectacular sunsets

SPORTS & ACTIVITIES

With a INSIDER TIP length of 2km/1.25 miles, the promenade around the lake behind the beach is the most pleasant jogging circuit on Phuket. Don't be too surprised when passing cars and mopeds sound their horns at the point where the road branches off to Cape Promthep. This is not directed at you, but a sign of respect for the Chinese shrine here. If you open the gate, you can enter the small building and light one of the joss sticks placed there free of charge.

WHERE TO STAY

THE ROYAL PHUKET YACHT CLUB ● ⛵

This hotel was built in the 1980s and is no longer the latest thing, but the location is still first-class. All rooms have a large terrace and a wonderful view of the bay. Because it is built on a slope, the hotel only has a small pool. The public road to Ao Sane passes directly beneath the hotel's Quarterdeck Restaurant. *110 rooms | Nai Harn Beach | tel. 076 38 02 00 | www.theroyalphuketyachtclub. com | Expensive*

ALL SEASONS

This resort is not right on the beach, but you only have to walk a few paces across the road. Comfortable rooms, two pools, sauna. *154 rooms | Nai Harn Beach | tel. 076 28 93 27, www.allseasons-naiharn-phuket.com | Expensive*

WHERE TO GO

LAEM PROMTHEP ★ ⛵
(116 B6) (*∅ C14*)

On this rocky cape, the southernmost tip of the island, whole busloads of tourists come to see the fantastic sunsets (access from Rawai and Nai Harn). From the cape *(laem)* you get a great view of the sea, the bay of Nai Harn and the island of Man. In the INSIDER TIP garden of the *Promthep Cape Restaurant (tel. 076 28 86 56 | Budget)* the *Phuket Paradise Cocktail* comes recommended. The food is okay but nothing special. Be sure to book a table with sea view! There are also stalls selling cooked meals and drinks at the cape.

In honour of the king, a ● *lighthouse (daily 10am–6pm)* was built. In the air-

RAWAI BEACH

(116 B–C6) (ꞔꞔ D14) **Rawai Beach has never been a tourist haunt. It is simply too muddy for most people, because the sea withdraws a long way at low tide. At least the sea cucumbers like the water here.**

Still, the beach used to be popular with

Fish straight from the sea is sold at the fish market on Rawai Beach

conditioned interior you can view marine charts, as well as models of ships and sextants. It's also well worth making the trip to the INSIDER TIP viewing point of the ⚘ *Promthep Alternative Energy Station* on the road from Nai Harn to the cape (take the turning by the wind generator).

long-term and permanent holidaymakers, as well as among the Thais themselves. In the village of Rawai time seemed to stand still, and it was possible to eat well and cheaply at the cooked-food stalls beneath the casuarina trees on the long beach – until progress arrived. A promenade (where almost nobody walks) was built and the food stalls were forced to move to the other end of the beach, where there is no shade, to the *Pakbang Food Center*. A four-lane road was then constructed through the middle of the village, robbing it of almost all its character.

FOOD & DRINK

BAAN HAD RAWAI
At the south end of Rawai Beach, Thai dishes and seafood are served in the open air. Many Thais come here to eat – which is always a good sign! *Daily | tel. 076 38 38 38 | Budget–Moderate*

FLINTSTONE
The rolls, bread and cakes from this bakery taste delicious. It also serves sandwiches with sausage and cheese, as well as good coffee. *Daily | beach road at the junction with the Phuket Town road | tel. 076 28 92 10 | Budget*

ENTERTAINMENT

The bars *Nikita* and *Freedom* are a favoured gathering point for the small numbers of tourists and the *falang* (expats) who live here permanently.

WHERE TO STAY

SIAM PHUKET RESORT
This resort has pleasant rooms, each with TV and minibar, in well-maintained grounds around a pool. *40 rooms | 24 Viset Rd. | tel. 076 28 89 47 | Moderate*

YA NUI BEACH

(116 B6) (*M C14*) **This is a picturesque little beach in a valley halfway between Nai Harn and Promthep.**

Even in the main season, the number of day trippers is not large.

WHERE TO STAY

INSIDER TIP ▶ **NAI YA BEACH BUNGALOWS**
Plain but attractive stilt bungalows with fans, five minutes up the hill beneath broad-leafed trees in well-kept grounds. Many long-term residents appreciate the peace and quiet here. The restaurant serves breakfast and snacks. *20 rooms | Open early Nov to end of April | 99 Soi Ya Nui | Viset Rd. | Rawai | tel. 076 28 88 17 | Budget*

LOW BUDGET

▶ The *Ao Sane Bungalows* in the bay of Ao Sane with their bamboo huts built on stilts are a reminder of the hippie era (300 baht with shower). Even the bungalows equipped with fans all cost less than 1000 baht. Many regular guests, sailors, excellent food. *23 rooms | Ao Sane | tel. 076 28 83 06*

▶ Breakfast for 30 baht: *Kanom Chin*, rice noodles with curry sauce, with raw and pickled vegetables and herbs are served in a nameless eatery *(Fri–Wed 7am–11am)*. When you come up from Nai Harn, turn left into Sai Yuan Rd. you'll find it on the right after approx. 150 metres/165 yds (opposite Didi's Hair Salon). But don't expect anyone to speak English here!

▶ *On The Rock*: rooms with fan or airconditioning for 800 to 1200 baht. Behind the *Yacht Club* resort. Two minutes' walk to Nai Harn Beach. *Tel. 08 69 52 08 19*

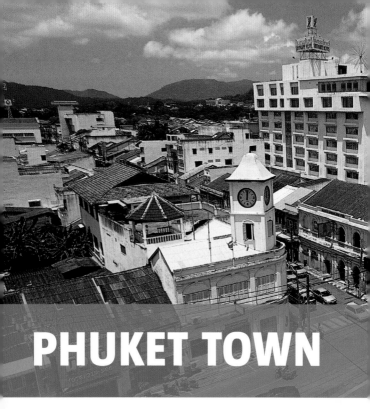

PHUKET TOWN

MAP INSIDE BACK COVER
(117 D–E 2–3) *(∅ E–F 10–11)*

While Phuket Town is the capital of the island province, it is far from being a provincial town.

Whereas in other districts the old wooden houses gave way to concrete blocks long ago, in *Old Phuket Town*, the centre of Phuket Town, many buildings in the so-called Sino-Portuguese style have remained. Showing the signs of time and the tropical climate, they contribute to the charm of this bustling town of 70,000 inhabitants.

Of course the modern construction boom and tourism have made their mark, and visitors who leave the beach for a few hours in the daytime to come to town often fail to notice that the old Phuket is still alive, only one street away from the faceless new buildings and souvenir shops. However, if you take a little time and look in the nooks and crannies, you will discover many details that add up to a likeable overall picture.

SIGHTSEEING

JUI TUI TEMPLE ★ ●
(U A3–4) *(∅ a3–4)*

This Chinese Taoist temple at the corner of Ranong Rd. and Soi Phu Thon is dedicated to the vegetarian god Kiu Wong and is the site of many ceremonies during the *Vegetarian Festival*. The roofs of next door's *Kwan Im Teng* (sometimes called *Put Jaw*), also a Taoist temple, are adorned with rampant dragons. It is dedicated to the

Old townhouses in the Sino-Portuguese style, lots of restaurants, folklore and a host of little shops – Phuket Town has plenty of variety

goddess of mercy, and dates back 200 years, which makes it Phuket's oldest Chinese temple. *Free admission*

OLD PHUKET TOWN ★ ●
(U B3) (*b3*)

No other city in Thailand possesses so much old architecture with colonial charm as Phuket Town. Chinese immigrants from neighbouring Malaysia brought the Sino-Portuguese style with them. North of the roundabout near to the central market, the old quarter is full

WHERE TO START?
Roundabout (U B3–4) (*b3–4*): Bangkok Rd., Ranong Rd., Yaowaraj Rd. and Rasada Rd. meet at the central roundabout. The public buses and pickups from the beaches arrive here. Go left to the market, head north and you'll soon find yourself in the middle of the old quarter. Going right will take you to the shopping district.

In Phuket's Soi Rommani, splendid townhouses have stood the test of time

of shop buildings with stucco decorations. The ground floors are for business, and whole families live above. In *Thalang Road* in particular you are strolling through the architectural history of the town. Fine examples of sensitive restoration of the old building fabric can be seen in the side street *Soi Rommani*. The imposing townhouses of the old tin magnates are to be found along *Krabi Road*, for example. The outstanding example here is *Phra Pitak Chinpracha Mansion*, which is over 100 years old. Following an elaborate restoration, it now houses the restaurant *Blue Elephant* (see p. 69).

ORCHID GARDEN & THAI VILLAGE
(115 D5) (*ØJ F10*)
Thai dancing, Thai boxing, Thai weddings – a great deal of folklore is on display here by this lake in a former tin mine. It is purely for tourist purposes, but entertaining all the same. The obligatory elephant rides are also on offer. The product range of the souvenir shops is produced here on the spot, and orchids bloom on an area of 1600 m²/17,000 sq ft. *Shows daily 11am and 5.30pm | admission 250 baht | on the northern edge of town,* *turn off left from the highway to the airport (signposted) | tel. 076 2148 60*

RANG HILL ★ ⛰ (U A1–2) (*ØJ a1–2*)
The Thai name for the hill that overlooks Phuket Town on its northwestern side is *Khao Rang* (access via *Kho Simbi Rd.* or *Soi Wachira*). Its height may be a modest 139 m/456 ft, but it commands a beautiful view of the whole town – and is home to a lot of monkeys. If the jogging trail to the top is not to your taste, try the excellent Thai food at the *Tung-Ka Café (tel. 076 2115 00 | Budget).*

SAM SAN TEMPLE (U A3) (*ØJ a3*)
Tien Sang Sung Moo, the goddess of the sea and patron of sailors and fishermen, is venerated in this *sanjao* (Chinese temple) on *Krabi Road*. The entrance gate with its artistic sculptures, Chinese characters and glowing colours is highly photogenic – and usually outlined against a blue sky. *Admission free*

THAIHUA MUSEUM ● (U B3) (*ØJ b3*)
Phuket's oldest Chinese school, dating from 1934, has been turned into a museum. Here you can see many historic

photos, exhibits and information about the Thai-Chinese history of Phuket Town. The building in Sino-Portuguese style is also worth seeing. *28 Krabi Rd. | Tue–Sun 11am–7pm | admission 200 baht | www.thaihuamuseum.com*

WAT SIREY ☆ (115 F6) (⌖ G10)

When you leave the town centre on Sri Suthat Rd. heading east, you are without noticing it on a causeway that leads to the small island of *Ko Sirey*. It is separated from the main island only by the narrow *klong* (canal) of *Tha Jeen*. Here the Buddhist *Wat Sirey* temple with a reclining Buddha 10m/33ft long crowns the top of a hill, from which you enjoy a fine view.

FOOD & DRINK

ANNA'S (U B4) (⌖ b4)

Stylish restaurant within restored historic walls. The Western food is mediocre, but the Thai dishes are authentic. *Daily lunch/dinner | 13 Rasada Rd. | near the roundabout | tel. 076 2105 35 | Budget–Moderate*

BAAN KLUNG JINDA RESTAURANT (U B3) (⌖ b3)

Enjoy Thai food in the stylish surroundings of a wonderful old townhouse. You can even celebrate your wedding here. *Daily | 158 Yaowaraj Rd. | tel. 076 2217 77 | www.baanklung.com | Moderate*

BLUE ELEPHANT ☆ (U B3) (⌖ b3)

This is the name of a chain of outstanding Thai restaurants in Europe and Asia. In the old quarter of Phuket the blue elephant has unpacked its trunk in an imposing townhouse that is more than 100 years old. Royal Thai cuisine at its very best. And in the restaurant's own school of cookery you can put on the chef's hat

yourself or try to carve a melon into a work of art. *Daily lunch/dinner | 96 Krabi Rd. | tel. 076 35 43 55 | www.blueelephant.com/phuket | Expensive*

LE CAFÉ (U B4) (⌖ b4)

This pleasant little bistro-style café serves Western and Thai meals. *Daily from 10am | 64/5 Rasada Centre | Rasada Rd. | Budget*

INSIDER TIP ▶ CHINA INN (U B3) (⌖ b3)

Charming restaurant in a lovingly restored Sino-Portuguese townhouse. The Thai food is authentic and delicious. *Mon–Sat | 20 Thalang Rd. | tel. 076 35 62 39 | Budget–Moderate*

HOKKIEN NOODLE SOUP (U B3) (⌖ b3)

Every day until late afternoon a tasty noodle soup is served in this basic eatery for less than a pound/around one US dollar. *At the roundabout near the market | Budget*

KA JOK SI
(U B4) (*b4*)

In this somewhat cramped but cosy historic townhouse with antique decorations you can sample excellent Thai cuisine that is good value for money. Later in the evening, when a ladyboy croons some songs and owner Mr Lek dances the tango, the diners sometimes get up on their chairs and applaud – or join in the dancing. *Tue–Sat dinner | 26 Takua Pa Rd. | tel. 076 21 79 03 | Moderate*

INSIDER TIP **SIAM INDIGO**
(U B3) (*b3*)

This carefully restored townhouse is a gem. First-class, authentic Thai food such as duck in a mild curry *(massaman)*. *Daily from 11am | 8 Phang Nga Rd. | tel. 076 25 66 97 | www.siamindigo.com | Moderate–Expensive*

LOW BUDGET

▶ The *Thavorn Hotel* will give you a room with a fan for 250 baht, and one with air-conditioning for 500 baht. The rooms are not very modern, but spacious (and those facing the street are noisy). Part of the old-world lobby has been designated a ● museum. *200 rooms | 74 Rasada Rd. | tel. 076 211 33 |*

▶ You can make phone calls for an unbeatably low price in the state-run *Communication Authority of Thailand (CAT)*: 2.5 baht per min. to phone home. *Mon–Fri 8am–8pm, Sat/Sun 8am–5pm | 112/2 Phang Nga Rd. (near the main post office)*

▶ Tasty dishes cost 100 baht at most here: For the best chicken & rice head for *Kota Khao Man Gai (Soi Surin | near Crystal Inn, opposite the orthopaedic clinic)*. Muslims like to eat murtabak and roti, a kind of pancake stuffed with chicken or vegetables, which tastes especially good at *Abdul* and *Aroon*. Both of these places occupy the upper end of *Thalang Rd., near Thepkrasattri Rd. (daily 6am–5.30pm)*.

SHOPPING

In the centre of Phuket Town one store follows the other along the main shopping streets: *Ranong, Rasada, Yaowaraj south, Montri* and *Tilok Uthit 1 Rd.* The largest shop in the town centre, with a supermarket, is *Robinson* on *Tilok Uthit 1 Rd.*, behind the Ocean Shopping Mall. The second-largest shopping centre on the island, *Central Festival*, lies on the edge of town on the road leading to Patong. In the evenings, Thais flock to the *night market* on *Ong Sim Phai Rd.*, mainly because of the food stalls.

INSIDER TIP **ISLAND PARADISE**
(U B3) (*b3*)

Small but excellent boutique. Selected items and accessories from the flimsiest beachwear to far-out belts. *8 Phang Nga Rd., next to Siam Indigo*

OLD PHUKET GALLERY ●
(U B3) (*b3*)

Old Phuket is shown in black-and-white photos in this historic townhouse. Many of the views are available as postcards. *74 Thalang Rd.*

INSIDER TIP ▶ OLDEST HERBS SHOP
(U B3) *(∭ b3)*

If you follow your nose in the old quarter, you cannot miss this traditional Chinese herbalist. It was opened in 1917 by the grandfather of the current owner, Mr Wiwan. Not much has changed in the shop since then. It smells of medicinal herbs,

the books are second-hand, but they are available in many languages, including English of course. *3 Phang Nga Rd.*

V. MULTI GEMS INTERNATIONAL
(U C3) *(∭ c3)*

This long-established jeweller's has a good reputation. The range of pearls,

The market stands are piled high with tempting exotic fruit and vegetables

as it has for generations. If you describe your ailment, the remedy to cure it will be prepared for you, without any chemical additives. *16 Thalang Rd.*

PRIVATE COLLECTION (U B3) *(∭ b3)*

Silk, jewellery and crafts from Kashmir and India in a beautifully restored townhouse. These are not your run-of-the-mill souvenirs, and therefore not cheap. *265 Yaowaraj Rd.*

SOUTHWIND BOOKS (U B3) *(∭ b3)*

You won't find a better selection of books and magazines on the whole island. All

precious stones and jewellery is enormous. You can also design items the way you want them and have them produced here, and watch jewellers and goldsmiths at work to learn how raw precious stones are cut. *154 Thepkrasattri Rd. | www.vmultigems.com*

INSIDER TIP ▶ WUA ART GALLERY
(U C3) *(∭ c3)*

Mr Zen is an artist who paints in a minimalist style, and is pleased to have a chat with visitors. He has designed his gallery as a complete work of art in itself. *95 Phang Nga Rd. | daily 10am–10pm*

Martial art with hands and feet: muay thai, Thai boxing, is the national sport

PEARL BOWLING (U C4) (🗺 c4)

The bowling alleys are next to the *Pearl Hotel*. In the afternoons you can chance your arm without booking in advance. *Daily from 2pm | Montri Rd. | tel. 076 2114 18*

ENTERTAINMENT

While most tourists prefer to look for entertainment in the beach bars, the locals like to go to the nightclubs, pubs, coffee shops and karaoke joints in town. However, there are some places where both Thais and *falang* with local knowledge can be found, for example in the rustic *Timber & Rock (118/1 Yaowaraj Rd.)*, where a rock band hottens things up every evening except Sunday from 9pm. In *Rockin Angels (daily 8pm–1am | 54 Yaowaraj Rd. | just before the junction with Thalang Rd.)* Patrick plays as a one-man band, and with ten customers inside the place is full. Resident *falang* meet up in *Michaels Bar (daily 11am–1am | Takua Pa Rd. www.phuket-town.com/michaels)* beneath the big screen or to play pool. Young, hip Thais like to dance at *Kor Tor Mor (daily 8pm–2am | 41/5 Chana Charoen Rd. | near Robinson)*. Live bands and DJs with a liking for hip-hop provide the sound.

Films are shown in English on several screens at the *Paradise Multiplex* on *Tilok Uthit Road* next to the Ocean Shopping Centre. Thai boxing is staged every Friday from 8pm in the *boxing stadium (Saphan Hin)* at the south end of *Phuket Road,* approx. 2 km/1.25 miles outside the centre.

WHERE TO STAY

In terms of value for money, the accommodation here is much better than on the beaches. As the island is not very large, staying in town is an option worth considering, for example to start off while you take a closer look at the beaches.

CRYSTAL INN (U C4) (🗺 c4)

A modern urban hotel that would cost at least twice as much for the same facilities near a beach. All rooms have air-conditioning, TV, minibar. Internet café. Central location. *54 rooms | 2/1–10 Soi*

Surin | Montri Rd. | tel. 076 25 67 89 |
www.phuketcrystalinn.com | *Budget*

ON ON HOTEL (U B3) (*ill b3*)

This 1920s establishment close to the centre of town is a part of movie history: as the most popular backpacker hostel in Phuket Town, it was a film location for The Beach with Leonardo DiCaprio. In summer 2012 the rooms, which had become extremely shabby, got a thorough renovation. *49 rooms | 19 Phang Nga Rd. | tel. 076 22 57 40 | Budget*

PEARL HOTEL (U C4) (*ill c4*)

Once the top address, now showing its age a bit, but it has all necessary amenities and a lovely small pool – as well as live music in the coffee shop in the evenings and an excellent Chinese restaurant on the premises. The massage salon is not an unusual feature in a Thai hotel and causes no annoyance. Central location. *250 rooms | 42 Montri Rd. | tel. 076 2110 44 | www.pearlhotel.co.th | Moderate*

ROYAL PHUKET CITY (U D4) (*ill d4*)

The best hotel in town, and good value for money. Gym, pool, sauna, spa. For the most delicious cakes in Phuket Town, head for the in-house INSIDER TIP ▶ Bistro *154. 251 rooms | 154 Phang Nga Rd. | opposite the bus station | tel. 076 23 33 33 | www.royalphuketcity.com | Moderate–Expensive*

THALANG GUESTHOUSE (U B3) (*ill b3*)

This accommodation occupies a 70-year-old townhouse. The basic rooms come equipped with a fan or air-conditioning. ☼ Two rooms on the top floor have a balcony with a great view of the town, and owner Mr Ti is extremely helpful. *12 rooms | 37 Thalang Rd. | tel. 076 2142 25 | www.talangguesthouse.com | Budget*

INFORMATION

TOURISM AUTHORITY OF THAILAND (TAT) (U C3) (*ill c3*)

Accommodation listings, transport timetables and brochures, including information from private service providers, are available here. *191 Thalang Rd. | tel. 076 2110 36 | tatphket@tat.or.th*

WHERE TO GO

BOAT LAGOON (115 D3) (*ill F8*)

Landlubbers are welcome in the Boat Lagoon, Phuket's oldest marina, with its restaurants, bars and cafés. For excellent Thai and Italian food, try Watermark *(daily from 12 noon | tel. 076 23 97 30 | www.watermarkphuket.com | Moderate–Expensive)*. The baked goods, cakes and chocolates for sale at r Patisserie are delightful. Oh yes, and you can buy or charter a yacht here (Thepkasattri Rd., approx. 10 km/6 miles north of Phuket Town, towards the airport).

PHUKET TIN MINING MUSEUM ● (115 D4) (*ill E9*)

Phuket was a prosperous island in days gone by, too. The money lay underground in those days: tin. This interesting museum presents the conditions in which the metal was extracted. There is even a complete reconstruction of a tunnel with life-size miners. The exhibitions tell you all about Phuket's tin-mining history, in a fine building in the Sino-Portuguese architectural style. Near Phuket Town but in a green environment, off the tourist track on the road that branches off from the highway to the British International School approx. 7 km/4.5 miles north of Phuket Town (just after the junction of by-pass 402 with the highway). The museum is approx. 1.5km/1 mile west of the school. *Mon–Sat 9am–4pm | admission 100 baht | tel. 076 32 2140*

DESTINATIONS AROUND PHUKET

Many islands surround Phuket, like emeralds lying on blue velvet. A few of them have sugar-white beaches, others are merely limestone rocks in strange shapes.

PHANG NGA BAY

(118 B3) *(⚏ G–H 1–2)* ★ **Phang Nga Bay northeast of Phuket is speckled with limestone islands and rocks. On some of the islands there are caves with stalactites and stalagmites, which can only be entered at low tide in a canoe or a longtail boat.**

In 1974 a scene for The Man with the Golden Gun was filmed here. In the background is *Ko Tapu*, 'Nail Island', which really does look like a nail driven into the sea thanks to the erosion of its rocky base by the waves.

Ko Pannyi is often wrongly marketed under the name *Sea Gypsy Island*. In fact the inhabitants of the houses built on stilts in shallow water at the foot of this huge rocky massif are Muslim families. The restaurants at the edge of the village are an obligatory port of call for all organised tours to Phang Nga. They are included in the programme of every travel agency, and go from Phuket by bus to Phang Nga and the pier of Tha Dan. Here boats await to take visitors through the bay. The journey time from the mainland bridge in the north of Phuket is ap-

Photo: On the Similan Islands in the Andaman Sea

This is a picture postcard – jungle and fine-grained sand, bizarrely shaped rocks and turquoise water …

proximately 50 minutes.

Alternatively you can set out on a boat trip directly from Phuket. Boats for Phang Nga Bay depart from the pier of *Ao Po* (113 E5) (*G5*) *(a one-day charter of a longtail costs approx. 4000 baht, spaces for eight passengers)*. A particularly romantic way to do the trip is to take one of the junks *June bahtra* and *Ayodhaya (day tour approx. 3500 baht, sunset trip approx. 2400 baht | book through travel agents or at www.phuket-travel.com/cruises)*.

The bay with rocks rising steeply from the water looks at its best in the gentle light of the rising sun or in the afternoon. If you would like to undertake the trip independently, you can stay the night below the pier of Tha Dan right by the water (not a swimming beach!) in the comfortable *Phang Nga Bay Resort (88 rooms | 20 Tha Dan Rd. | tel. 076 41 20 67 | Moderate)* and then charter a longtail at the pier. The day trip costs approx. 4000 baht, and eight people fit into the boat.

One of the most popular postcard motifs in Thailand: from the viewpoint on Ko Phi Phi

KO LONE

(116–117 C–D 5–6) *(◫ E–F 13–14)* **Although it is only 15 minutes from the pier in Chalong, this mountainous jungle island, inhabited only by a few fishermen and rubber tappers, is a natural paradise for those in search of peace and quiet.**

WHERE TO STAY

CRUISER ISLAND RESORT

Attractive bungalows with air-conditioning and TV. Pool, tennis court. The environmentally aware management promotes recycling and protection of the corals. Booking office in *Rawai (Soi Sermsuk | Viset Rd.)*, *tel. 076 383210 | www.cruiserislandresort.com* | Expensive

KO PHI PHI

(117 E–F 5–6) *(◫ G–H 13–14)* ★ **On a list of the world's most beautiful islands, Ko Phi Phi would have a good chance of taking one of the top places.**

The island consists of green mountains submerged in the sea, with dramatic rock formations and beaches to die for, surrounded by waters that are among the best in the world for diving and snorkelling. Paradise has a downside, however. Following the tsunami the opportunity for reconstruction was not taken by planners. Almost every square metre that could be built on in the island village or Tonsai *(Ban Laem Trong)* has been put to use. Thousands of day trippers, who come on the fleet of ferries from Phuket, Krabi and Lanta, crowd the narrow streets of the centre. Holidaymakers who stay overnight on Ko Phi Phi don't have the island to themselves until the afternoon. They include many young people who like to party – and are not aware that they are staying in a Muslim village. *www.phi-phi.com | www.phiphihotels.info | www.phiphi.phuket.com | www.gophiphi.com*

SIGHTSEEING

VIEWPOINT ● (117 F6) *(◫ H14)*

Behind Tonsai Village it's a half-hour walk up a steep but maintained path to the viewpoint. At the top, ice-cold drinks are served and you can admire one of the most popular postcard views in all Thailand. If you prefer not to go back the same way, you can descend in about 20 minutes through the woods on an extremely steep, unpaved path to INSIDER TIP *Ran Ti Bay* which has a few

basic bungalows, as well as longtails that can take you back to the village.

FOOD & DRINK

The numerous restaurants in the island's little village serve Thai food and seafood, but also international dishes. The best address is *Le Grand Bleu (Moderate)*. Fresh baguettes with ham and cheese can be had from the *Pee Pee Bakery (Budget)*.

SPORTS & ACTIVITIES

More than a dozen diving bases compete on Phi Phi. This keeps prices low and offers a good choice to the diving community.

ENTERTAINMENT

In several rustic bars and open-air pubs, partying in the village goes on into the small hours. The trendy place is *Carlitos Bar*. *Hippies Bar* and *Apache* are other favourite haunts for night owls.

WHERE TO STAY

In the main season – especially around New Year – this island is crowded. Advance booking is essential. And bear in mind that this island is bursting with visitors, which means you don't get the best value for money.

INSIDER TIP GARDEN INN BUNGALOW (117 F6) (*Ⓜ H14*)

The wooden bungalows and rooms in a guesthouse with air-conditioning or a fan are basic but well kept. Lush greenery in the garden, five minutes from the beach of Lo Dalam. *9 rooms | at the end of the village, to the right of the ascent to the viewpoint | tel. 08 17 87 43 51 | www.krabidir.com/gardeninnbungalow | Budget–Moderate*

PHITAROM (117 F6) (*Ⓜ H14*)

Extremely comfortable bungalow rooms on a slope, all equipped with air-conditioning, TV and refrigerator. At the far end of the village on Lo Dalam Bay. Pool. *52 rooms | tel. 075 60 11 21 | www.phiphiresortphitarom.com | Expensive*

MARCO POLO HIGHLIGHTS

★ **Phang Nga Bay**
Where limestone rocks rise from the sea → p. 74

★ **Ko Phi Phi**
Film set: twin islands of the kind adored by Hollywood → p. 76

★ **Ko Raya Yai**
A hilly jungle in the sea with superb beaches → p. 79

★ **Ko Similan**
A colourful underwater world in one of the top diving destinations on the planet → p. 79

★ **Ko Yao Noi**
Where hornbills fly – a relaxing green island → p. 80

KO PHI PHI

WHERE TO GO

Boat tours including a lunch box and snorkelling gear for a fixed price are on offer everywhere. You can charter a long-

hewn from rock. It is worth taking a look at the *Viking Cave*. The origin of the rock paintings, which are reminiscent of Viking ships, is dubious, but the bamboo poles hanging from the roof of the cave

A film set and stunning rocky scenery: Maya Bay on Ko Phi Phi Le

tail for a fixed price. Signs with information and prices at the pier.

INSIDER TIP KO MAI PAI
(118 C5) (*ω j5*)

Day trippers seldom set foot on *Bamboo Island*, as Ko Mai Pai is also known, as this flat, tiny island is most suitable for those visitors to Phi Phi who have plenty of time. The water and the beach could not be more attractive.

KO PHI PHI LE (118 C6) (*ω j6*)

The small *(le)* uninhabited sister island of Phi Phi Don (*don* meaning large) rises from the deep-blue sea like a castle

are definitely genuine. Bold collectors of swallows' nests use them to climb up and pluck off the spittle-glued nests of salangan swallows.

Phi Le Bay is a stunning rocky cove with turquoise-coloured water. *Maya Bay* even surpasses it: walls of limestone rise from the water to heights of up to 200m/650ft, forming a breathtaking natural arena. The Beach with Leonardo DiCaprio was filmed here. Rangers patrol the beach and charge all foreigners 200 baht admission to the national park. It is best to come here in the morning or late afternoon, when things are quieter!

KO RAYA YAI

(118 A6) *(🗺 g6)* ⭐ A few fishermen's families, beach bars and eight resorts share this mountainous green island with snowy-white beaches. Although day trippers do visit, you can get the perfect island feeling here.

And if you want real tranquillity, simply take a 15-minute walk to the other side of the island. Tours to Raya (also spelled Racha) are on offer at every travel agent's. Speedboats make the crossing from Chalong pier in 40 minutes. They can take about 20 passengers *(return trip approx. 1500 baht)*.

WHERE TO STAY

BUNGALOW RAYA RESORT 🍃
Plain bungalows with shower and fan (the power goes off at midnight) on a slope with a fantastic view. The resort also has a good restaurant right by the sea. *20 rooms | tel. 076 35 20 87 | www.bungalowraya.com | Moderate*

THE RACHA 🕙
This stunningly beautiful resort on a wonderful white beach offers environmentally sound accommodation in villas. As few trees as possible were felled to build it – and for every one that was chopped down, two new trees were planted. Palms are allowed to grow through the roofs wherever possible. Most waste is recycled, and the beach is cleaned daily. Guests at the resort have to share it with daytrippers, however. Two pools, tennis court, gym and spa. *85 rooms | office in Chalong close to the pier | tel. 076 35 54 55 | www.theracha.com | Expensive*

KO SIMILAN

(0) *(🗺 0)* ⭐ These nine jungle-covered rocky islands 110 km/70 miles north-west of Phuket are uninhabited and have only a few small sandy beaches.

It is what lies underwater that makes them so fascinating. The Similans are among the world's top diving destinations. At visibility of up to 30 m/100 ft, divers and snorkellers have the chance to see big fish such as whale sharks and mantas as well as a sensational display of corals. All the diving stations offer trips to the Similans lasting several days on motor yachts or sailing yachts. Travel agencies also run day trips for snorkellers and tours including an overnight stay on island no. 4. Minibuses depart from Phuket for Taplamu on the mainland (approx. two hours). From there, the crossing by speedboat to Similan takes about 1.5 hours. The islands are a 🕙 national park *(admission 200 baht)*, and the park authority makes accommodation in bungalows or tents available for overnight guests *(www.dnp.go.th)*. During the

LOW BUDGET

▶ The bungalows at *P. P. Nice Beach* are spartan, but have a fan and shower. From 800 baht. At the quiet west end of Tonsai Bay behind the hospital. *16 rooms | tel. 08 94 51 64*

▶ Rooms for 800 baht right on the beach? Baan Tha Khao Bungalows *(tel. 076 58 27 33 | www.kohyaobun galow.com)* on Ko Yao Noi fit the bill. And for 500 baht per day you can rent a kayak.

monsoon season from early May until late October the park is closed.

KO YAO NOI

(118 B4) (∅ h4) ⭐ **The second-largest island in the bay of Phang Nga is a green gem in the sea that can be reached by ferry from Phuket in half an hour – yet few tourists find their way here. The reason is that Ko Yao Noi has no wonderful beaches, and the water recedes a long way at low tide.**

But this is a blessing! The island, populated by 4000 Muslim farmers and fishermen, has retained its authentic charm. It is a perfect spot for relaxing and enjoying the natural surroundings. Ferries go several times daily from Phuket (Bang Rong pier on the east coast) and from Krabi Province (Thalane pier).

FOOD & DRINKS

In the island's main settlement, which is simply named 'Talad' (market), Dora from Denmark and Stephane from France serve not only fish but also real Thai coffee and cocktails in their likeable INSIDER TIP *Je t'aime (tel. 076 59 74 95 | Budget–Moderate)*. On the ring road just before Pasai Beach a German from Berlin dishes up steak and sautéed potatoes at *Rice Paddy (tel. 076 45 42 55 | Budget–Moderate)*, which you can follow up with cappuccino ice-cream for dessert. Also on the ring road, just before Takhao Bay, Romano from Italy, at *La Luna (tel. 08 46 29 15 50 | www.lalunakohyao.com | Budget–Moderate)*, bakes fresh pizza in his oven. At *Pasai Seafood (tel. 08 72 64 12 81 | Budget–Moderate)* on the beach of the same name you can enjoy Thai meals and seafood right on the beach.

SHOPPING

Small shops on the beaches and the ring road sell essential items. The main village has a few shops catering to daily needs and the island's only air-conditioned *7-Eleven* shop, but it sells no alcohol. However, there is a cash machine at 7-Eleven from which you can withdraw money using your credit card. The *Wine Shop* next to the *Je t'aime* restaurant stocks a selection of wines and spirits.

SPORTS & ACTIVITIES

Many resorts and tour operators hire out kayaks and organise tours to the islands in the bay of Phang Nga. You can also hire a bike and set off on the good but quiet island ring road, to explore a large part of Ko Yao Noi in about 1.5 hours. The island is home to many birds, and even the rare hornbill can be seen here. INSIDER TIP ▶ Ornithologist Mr Bay leads guided walks for bird-watchers. Contact him through *Ulmar's Nature Lodge (tel. 076 58 27 28)* in Takhao Bay. This is also the site of the pavilion where ● *Island Yoga (tel. 08 46 90 37 31 | www.thailand yogaretreats.com)* holds its yoga sessions. Ko Yao Noi and the surrounding islets with their limestone cliffs are an El Dorado for climbers. The team from *Ko Yao Rock Climbing (Thakhao Bay | tel. 08 48 41 15 40 | www.themountainshop.org)* will take you there. For underwater activities, contact *Koh Yao Diver (base in the Lom Lae Beach Resort on the southern part of the east coast | tel. 076 59 74 06 | kohyaodiver.com)*. You can learn self-defence using hands and feet at the *KYN Gym in Lamsai village | by the Lamsai Village Hotel | tel. 08 22 89 42 76 | www. phuket-krabi-muaythai.com)*. The instructors are a former Thai champion named Hlukhin and a professional woman boxer,

Lisa from England. In the main settlement on the island, Mrs Mina's *Tappee Thai Cookery Class (tel. 08 78 87 31 61)* shows you how to make curry and other dishes.

WHERE TO STAY

Almost all accommodation runs along the beaches of the east coast, which are accessed via the ring road. About a dozen resorts, most of them basic, cater for guests. Six Senses, by contrast, is an absolutely top-class haven, one of the most exclusive resorts in southern Thailand.

KOYAO ISLAND RESORT ☺

High prices, but no air-conditioning or TV? This is all deliberate here. The cabins with an area of up to 120 m² /1300 sq ft were built in the traditional way, largely from natural materials (even the bathtubs are wooden) that do not retain heat but let the air circulate and fit in perfectly with the palm forest by the sea. This is an eco-resort of the very finest quality with two pools. *22 rooms | Klong Jark Beach | tel. 076 59 74 74 | www.koyao. com | Expensive*

NAM TOK BUNGALOW

'Take it easy' says the sign at the entrance. In the restaurant you can sway in a hammock, and the rustic bungalows with air-conditioning or a fan will take you back to the hippie days. A lovely spot for chilling out. *15 rooms | Takhao Bay | tel. 08 52 58 78 24 | www.namtokbungalow.com | Budget–Moderate*

SABAI CORNER

The veteran amongst the resorts on Koy Yao is beautifully located beneath trees on a slope next to the sea. Wooden bungalows with fans, roofed with palm fronds, of various sizes: you can rent a house sleeping five. Cosy restaurant. *12 rooms | Klong Jark Beach | tel. 076 59 74 97 | www.sabaicornerbungalows. com | Budget–Moderate*

SIX SENSES ☺

In this upmarket resort, the houses are mainly built from natural materials too,

Ko Yao Noi is just right for travellers who want peace and quiet

Luxury without ostentation and ecological awareness characterise Six Senses

and the bedrooms are air-conditioned. This is luxury without ostentation, right down to the last detail, including an additional refrigerator for wine. The grounds slope down from a jungle-covered hill to the sea, where in the evenings films are screened on the small private beach. Guests can explore the mangrove forest next door on boardwalks. Herbs, fruit and salad vegetables are grown in the resort's own garden, waste is composted, and no plastic bottles are used here. Pool, spa, gym, tennis court. *50 rooms | between Klong Jark Beach and Takhao Bay | tel. 076 418500 | www.six senses.com/sixsensesyaonoi | Expensive*

INSIDER TIP SUNTISOOK RESORT

A family-run business, where guests feel at home. Manager Chui looks after everything and cooks with her mother – mashed potatoes too! Spacious bungalows with air-conditioning, TV, refrigerator or fan in a well-kept garden. You cross a very quiet road to get to the beach. *9 rooms | Takhao Bay | tel. 076 582750 | Budget–Moderate*

KO YAO YAI

(118 B4–5) (∅ h4–5) The larger of the two Yao islands is twice as big and twice as long (approx. 25 km/15 miles) as its little sister. Tourism is not even in its infancy here – it is just being born.

Outside the ten resorts there is hardly any tourist infrastructure on this island with its seven villages. It is just right for nature lovers in search of tranquillity who would like to experience authentic, rural island life. Most of the 12,000 inhabitants live in the south of the island, which can be reached daily by ferry from Phuket harbour or the Bang Rong pier. The boats to Ko Yao Noi stop at the north of the island on the way. For information on Ko Yao Yai see the websites given for Kao Yao Noi.

FOOD & DRINK

At the pier of Loh Jark Pier in the south of the island you can eat grilled chicken and spicy papaya salad at cooked-food stalls with a sea view. On the access road to the pier, the *Bua Siam restaurant (Budget)* actually lists its Thai dishes on an English-language menu.

SHOPPING

A concrete road runs the length of the island from north to south. Scattered along it are small shops that sell food and everyday items. Most of the shops are to be found in the south at the main settlement by the pier.

SPORTS & ACTIVITIES

The main road, which has very little traffic, and the two roads or tracks that branch off it to the beaches are ideal for mountainbikers. Most of the resorts hire out bikes and mopeds. Mr Virote, manager of the *Activities Resort (main road in the south of the island | tel. 076 58 24 75 | www.kohyaooactivitiesresort.com)* not only has bungalows, but also runs ☺ ecological tours, e.g. INSIDER TIP kayak trips through the mangroves at full moon, as well as horse-riding through the forests and countryside, and to the beaches. *Elixir Divers (in the Elixir Resort | tel. 08 78 97 00 76 | www.elixirdivers. com)* is the island's only diving base.

WHERE TO STAY

ELIXIR RESORT

Luxurious bungalows roofed with palm straw in an extensive garden right by the beach. This is the best accommodation at the south end of the island. With pool and gym. *31 rooms | Loh Yark Bay | tel. 08 78 08 38 38 | www.elixirresort.com | Expensive*

INSIDER TIP ▶ HEIMAT GARDENS

Yamalia brings a touch of the Alps to Thailand: she was born on Ko Yao Yai, but lived in the part of German-speaking Tyrol that belongs to Italy. The clean rooms with air-conditioning, TV, refrigerator and balcony in a terraced house are good value for money. It is a five-minute walk to the almost deserted beach of Lo Paret. Yamalia also organises tours. *5 rooms | south of the island | turn-off from the main road to Lo Paret Beach | tel. 08 57 94 74 28 | www.heimatgardens.com | Budget*

KO YAO YAI VILLAGE ☺

Surrounded by rubber trees and rainforest, the bungalows have a roof of palm straw and a canopy of leaves above. A natural environment, but no need to forego creature comforts. Vegetables are grown in the garden. Gym, spa with sauna, big pool with a fantastic view of Phang Nga Bay. At low tide the sea goes out a long way, and the beach is rocky. *49 rooms | north of the island | tel. 076 58 45 00 | www.kohyaoyaivillage.com | Expensive*

YAO YAI BEACH RESORT

Bungalows on stilts in a garden right by the sea, with cladding of bamboo mats and a thatched roof, with air-conditioning or fan. All have TV and refrigerator. *19 rooms | Lo Paret Beach | south of the island | tel. 08 19 68 46 41 | www.yaoyai resort.com | Budget--Moderate*

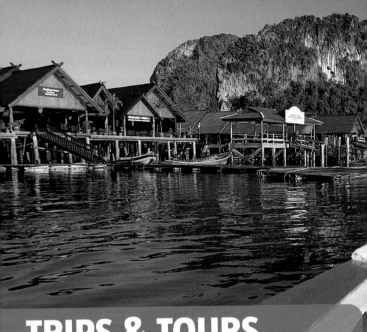
Photo: Bay of Phang Nga

TRIPS & TOURS

The tours are marked in green in the road atlas,
pull-out map and on the back cover

① WALKING WITH A VIEW

Walking along the beaches on Phuket is not especially pleasurable. Traffic is normally heavy, and pavements are few and far between. But in the most scenic part of the island, far in the south, there is a route on which you can walk more or less undisturbed from one beach to another with spectacular views and wonderful spots for relaxing on the way, Taking into account some breaks, reckon on taking a day for the distance of about 12 km/7.5 miles.

The excursion starts with a visit to a monastery. On the approach road to Nai Harn Beach → p. 62 you will see a large car park on the left just before you reach the beach. From here you can enter **Wat Nai Harn**. In this haven of peace it is easy to forget that holiday-makers from all over the world are sunbathing on a dream beach just a few paces away. When you stroll through the monastery grounds, look out for a huge INSIDER TIP banyan tree just to the left of the path. An odd collection of little shrines, dried garlands of flowers, dolls, miniature elephants and other votive offerings on its trunk have been left here by visitors to the monastery who came to ask for wishes to be fulfilled – or to give thanks for the fulfilment of their requests.

The elaborately decorated central temple building with its glass mosaics glit-

Walking in the south, taking a hire car through the jungle, or cycling round an island – there are many ways to get moving

tering in the sun is also worth looking at. You can't miss the path to the back gate of the monastery. When you have passed through it, a promenade lined by trees leads around **Nai Harn Lake** in front of you. Bear right. After about 200 m/200 yd don't forget to turn around and take a photo of the temple, which is reflected in the water of the lake.

Continue by the lake until you reach a small **Chinese shrine**, and take the right fork towards Cape Promthep. This is a

quiet road, with woodland to the left and right, and you feel you are walking through the jungle. The road ascends in curves until, high above the sea, you get a glimpse of Nai Harn Beach through the vegetation and a bird's eye view of the lake there.

But the best view is yet to come! When the wind generator of the **Promthep Alternative Energy Station** → p. 64 appears in front of you, take the path that branches off to the right, and after only a few paces you will see a

INSIDER TIP viewing platform high above the sea. The panorama of the bay, flanked by green hills with an uninhabited island in the middle, is stunning.

Back on the road, you now descend to sea level. The little beach of Ya Nui → p. 65 is a good place for a swim, and if you have your mask and snorkel with you, take the opportunity to admire the corals and fish below the surface. From Ya Nui a road goes off left towards Rawai. Here too there is little traffic, but lots of greenery to the left and right. After about 1.5 km/1 mile you will reach the road that rises from Rawai to Cape Promthep. Bear left here and then right across the bridge. You can walk along Rawai Beach → p. 64 on the promenade. From here many motorboats take trippers to the outlying islands. A whole row of restaurants and stalls along the road serve seafood.

From Rawai return to the bridge and cross it, then follow the road that branches off right. It will take you past rubber plantations, as well as a lot of resorts, restaurants and houses. After approx. 2 km/1.25 miles it reaches the road to Sai Yuan. By going left, you will return to Nai Harn Beach. However, if you turn right here, a special treat lies in store. The traffic is noticeably heavier, but you can use the pavement on the left side of the road lined with shops and restaurants. Keep walking, until just past the Italian restaurant Da Vinci → p. 62 you see a sign marked **INSIDER TIP** Herbal Steam Sauna (daily 10am–8pm /sauna 50 baht, massage 300 baht). The facilities here are basic but serve their purpose. After a sauna you can lie down and have a massage beneath a roof of palm fronds. Afterwards a cup of coffee and one of the delicious cakes from the charming café A Spoonful of Sugar → p. 62 on the other side of the road go down very well. On the way back you can avoid the traffic by taking the road that goes off to the right opposite the German Bakery → p. 62. You will then walk in a big loop through green scenery, past resorts and private residences, until you reach Nai Harn Lake and the beach once again.

2 TO THE SOUTH OF THAILAND

This route for travellers keen to discover the mainland passes through the loveliest scenery in southern Thailand. You will explore the wonderful world of islands in the bay of Phang Nga, drive a hire car on good roads through lonely jungle, and walk on long beaches. The total distance covered is only a little over 300 km/190 miles, but with overnight stops you should plan on spending three or four days on the trip.

Highway 402 leads over Thepkrasattri Bridge to the mainland, meeting, in Khok Kloi, Highway 4 which you take in the direction of Phang Nga. 30 km/20 miles past Khok Kloi a little road veers off left to the beautifully situated monastery Wat Suwan Khuha and the cave of **INSIDER TIP** Tham Yai, where you can discover many Buddha statues. Return to the highway, and turn off left 3 km/2 miles before you reach Phang Nga Town to get to the pier of Tha Dan and the Phang Nga Bay Resort → p. 75. From here you can explore this wonderful bay with mangrove jungle, limestone mountains and caves at your own pace. If you think the scenery of mountains in the sea looks like a film set, you are right: The Man with the Golden Gun was filmed here. Hunting the villain, Roger Moore as James Bond zoomed across the water and even gave his name to a rocky islet

A flower with a diameter of nearly three feet: Rafflesia in Kao Phra Thaeo National Park

(James Bond Island). This bay is truly enchanting in the early morning light before hordes of tourists arrive from Phuket, or at sunset when most visitors have left again. If you charter a longtail boat at the pier, you can decide for yourself at what time you want to depart. Accommodation is available in **Ko Pannyi**, a Muslim village built on piles, in the basic but pleasant **INSIDERTIP** ▶ **Sayan Bungalows** run by the Yaowapa family *(contact via Sayan Tours | Phang Nga bus station | tel. 076 43 03 48 | www.sayantour.com)*. The next day, continue on Highway 4. At **Bang Ba**, road no. 4090 branches off left towards **Takua Pa**. After 50 km/30 miles through wild, impressive mountain and jungle scenery, east of Takua Pa you reach Highway 401 in the direction of **Surat Thani**. After 15 minutes on this road you will see the sign for ★ **Khao**

Sok National Park *(www.khaosok.com)* on the left. At 646 km²/250 sq miles, this park is the largest area of jungle in the south of Thailand. Tigers and wild elephants are said to roam the rainforest still, but it is highly unlikely that you will see one of them. However, you may well hear, and with a little luck see, one of the noisiest inhabitants of the jungle – gibbons sometimes put in an appearance near the overnight accommodation. Khao Sok National Park is home to more than 300 species of birds, including hornbills and kingfishers. You can even spot the world's biggest flower here: the bloom of Rafflesia can reach a diameter of up to one metre/three feet. The walking trails close to the park headquarters are well signposted, and guides show you the way through the dense vegetation on longer tours. It is definitely

Sleep by the river but high up in the trees – at the Rainforest Resort

worthwhile making a trip to the reservoir of **Cheow Larn**, where you can spend the night in a room on a raft. There is no need to fear malaria! It is advisable to have protection against mosquitoes (spray, long-sleeved shirt, socks), especially in the evening and after rainfall, but the area is regarded as being free of malaria. One accommodation option is the **Rainforest Resort** *(12 rooms | tel. 077 39 51 35 | www.krabidir.com/khaosokrainforest | Budget–Moderate)*. The bungalows and tree houses of **Our Jungle House** *(13 rooms | tel. 08 14 17 05 46 | www.krabidir.com/ourjunglehouse | Budget–Moderate)* also occupy a beautiful location. The resorts organise canoe tours and jungle trekking. A fun way to travel by water is INSIDERTIP tubing – a leisurely float down the **Sok River** in a truck tyre. On the way back to Phuket (approx. two hours driving time), south of the provincial town of **Takua Pa**, Highway 4 takes you past the endless beaches of **Khao Lak**. Of all the regions of southern Thailand, this area suffered most from the tsunami. However, nothing more can be seen of the devastation, and many new resorts and hotels welcome guests here. *www.khaolak.de | www.mykhaolak.de*

For a lovely view of the sea, sandy beaches and jungle-covered mountains, go to the ☆ **Khao Lak View Restaurant** *(Budget)*, right on the highway, which winds up a hill here at the southern end of the beach. From this point you only have to drive a further 75 km/45 miles south back to Phuket.

3 CYCLING AROUND AN ISLAND

The thinly populated island of Ko Yao Noi with its good, quiet ring road (approx. 25 km/16 miles) and tracks is a paradise if you like to move on two wheels.

Mountainbikes can be hired in many resorts, e.g. at **Suntisook** → p. 82 in Takhao Bay. Right by the water on the pier at Takhao you can enjoy a cup of coffee in the morning peace before you pedal off. First of all, pass through the small village towards the island's interior, which above all means climbing. You'll quickly realise that this is a hilly island. But if you have to go slowly for a few hundred metres, you will enjoy the view of green valleys and hills, jungle and rubber plantations all the more.

From the highest point on the road, a long straight stretch descends again to the main settlement on the island, Talad (market). Here you can leave your bike and take a stroll along the main street with its little shops. From the **Je t'aime** → p. 80 restaurant at the crossroads in the heart of Talad you can watch the easy pace of life here while cooling off with a drink and a piece of cake. Then continue, passing the post office, police station and school, and heading southeast. It is not long before you are in green countryside again. Here and there you pass a house or shop. In some places you also pedal through mangrove forests close to the coast. Don't be alarmed if a monitor lizard or a snake crosses the road in front of you.

In the far south of the island, a dead-end road branches off from the circular road towards Lamsai. Pass the Lamsai Village Hotel and continue cycling along the coast until the concrete road turns into a track and then ends. Here in a rustic restaurant in the water called **INSIDER TIP** **Lobster Sea Food** *(Budget)* you can eat fish on the wooden planks. Back on the road round the island, head to the right and after a short distance go right again onto a track. This leads to the Lom Lae Beach Resort *(www.lomlae.com)* on a lovely beach where you can swim even at low tide.

The circular road takes you on to Pasai Beach, where several resorts, shops, restaurants and food stalls serve snacks and meals right on the beach. Even in the high season it is quite possible that you will find no more than a dozen guests eating here. If your legs are getting tired by now, you can have a massage on the beach. And if it's time to exercise your arms, then hire a kayak to paddle up and down the shore.

The bike tour now leads along the east coast, accompanied by a sea view all the while. The recommendation for the next stop is the pleasant restaurant in the **Sabai Corner** → p. 81 resort, where the menu lists such exotic combinations as potato salad with tuna. On the return stretch to Takhao Bay there is only one more ascent to manage. It starts where a little road branches off to the **Six Senses** → p. 81 luxury resort, which doesn't really welcome trippers. The climb through the forest is over after approx. 100 m/100 yd, and then you can freewheel all the way down to **La Luna** → p. 80, where Roberto will serve you the cappuccino or espresso that you so richly deserve.

A little further on you pass through a rubber plantation, where the shining sea is already visible straight ahead. To round off the trip, how about a walk along the beach looking for shells? And if the tide is out, you can even get to a little rocky island on foot.

SPORTS & ACTIVITIES

If you want to do sports on holiday, you've come to the right place. On Phuket you can get up close and personal with whale sharks, ride through the rainforest on the back of an elephant, go water-skiing or paddle a canoe through a world of wonderful islands.

Most of the operators named below organise numerous and varied tours. Make your booking via the websites or through travel agents on the spot.

CANOE TOURS

The bay of Phang Nga east of Phuket is a wonderful area for canoeing. Among the highlights are caves (hong) into which you can paddle at low tide. Canoe tours on the tidal rivers and in the mangrove forests of Krabi Province east of Phuket or on the reservoir in the Khao Sok National Park are also delightful. *Paddle Asia (www.paddleasia.com) | Sea Canoe Thailand (www.seacanoe.net) | Sea Cave Canoe (www.seacavecanoe.com)*.

CLIMBING

The limestone cliffs of the islands in the bay of *Phang Nga* and on *Ko Phi Phi* are a delight for climbers. A day's course costs approx. 1,900 baht. On *Ko Yao Noi* courses are run by *Ko Yao Rock Climbing (www.themountainshop.org)*, on *Phi Phi* by *Spidermonkey Climbing (www.spidermonkeyclimbing.com)*.

Photo: Canoe tour in Khao Sok National Park

Deep in the jungle, below the waves or at the kitchen stove – Phuket is paradise for active holidays

COOKERY COURSES

How do you get a curry nice and creamy? What puts the spice into prawn soup? Many resort cook will demonstrate these secrets to their guests. Restaurants and independent cookery schools also organise courses, which can last one day or several days *(www.phuket.com/dining/index_cooking.htm)*.

DIVING

The Andaman Sea around Phuket is among the best diving areas in the whole world. With visibility of up to 30 m/100 ft you can watch enormous (and harmless) whale sharks or kaleidoscope swarms of coral fish. The uninhabited *Similan* Islands north of Phuket are a highlight. Less well known, but also excellent for divers, are the waters around INSIDER TIP ▶ *Ko Surin* north of Similan. Near the underwater reef of *Richelieu*

Rock the chances of seeing whale sharks and rays are very good.

The INSIDER TIP coral-covered underwater *Burma Banks* 165 km/100 miles northwest of the Similan Islands are in Burmese waters. This is where experienced divers can make genuinely new discoveries, and see many reef sharks and sharks of the high seas. Only one hour by boat from Phuket, around the Phi Phi Islands, and further south in the archipelago that extends down to the Malaysian border, a rich variety of underwater fauna and flora awaits.

The best season for diving, with calm waters, is January to April. A day trip including two dives costs approx. 2600 baht, a four-day diving trip to Similan or Surin approx. 22,600 baht. For a diving course of three to four days, expect to pay around 11,300 baht. You will find diving schools on Phuket, Phi Phi and both of the Yao Islands (www. tauchbasen.net). On Ko Phi Phi in particular there is one diving shop next to another. The competition is keen, which keeps prices down. Links to diving schools and tour operators can be found on the website of the state tourist organisation: *www.tourismthailand.org*.

GOLF

Seven golf courses make Phuket the top destination in Thailand for international golf tourism. Green fees start at approx. 2600 baht. The cheapest place to play a round is the INSIDER TIP nine-hole *Phunaka Golf Course* (www.phunakagolf.com) near Chalong *(from approx. 950 baht)* – and it is even open at night, with the course illuminated by floodlights. The caddies on Phuket (as in all of Thailand) are women. Arrangements for reduced green fees can be booked through: *Golf Orient (www.golforient.com) | Phuket Golf*

(www.phuket-golf.com) | *Phuket Golf Master (www.phuketgolf.net)*.

JUNGLE TOURS

Only one patch of rainforest remains on Phuket: the *Kao Phra Kaeo* reserve in the northeast. Two hours by car to the northeast of Phuket, however, in the *Khao Sok National Park (www.khaosok.com)*, tigers and wild elephants still occupy a huge area of jungle. A tour on foot, on the back of an elephant or by kayak through the jungle is an unforgettable experience. Operators: *Phuket Tours (www.phuket-travel.com) | Phuket Safari (www.phuket-safari-travel.com) | Siam Safari (www.siamsafari.com)*. You can also organise a trip to this national park independently without difficulties, getting there by hire car or on a public bus from Phuket Town.

MOUNTAINBIKING

Cycling over rough tracks and terrain is a new activity on Phuket. You can book half-day tours to explore the south and northeast of the island on tracks and the quieter roads. For a day tour, take a ferry over to *Ko Yao Noi*. Here more and more resorts hire out mountainbikes to their guests. Tours lasting two days often go east to the neighbouring provinces *Phang Nga* and *Krabi*. Tours can be booked through travel agents or directly with the organisers: *Action Holidays Phuket (www.biketoursthailand.com) | Siam Bike Tours (www.siambiketours. com). Sea Canoe Thailand (www.seaca noe.net)* also runs mountainbike tours.

SAILING

The islands of the ● Andaman Sea are heaven for sailors, and Phuket with its big marinas is the sailing centre of Asia. You can charter a yacht from several different companies. The costs for a day's charter without a skipper start at around 13,200 euros. Some yacht owners will take paying passengers on the long voyage to Europe or on a trip to the islands between Phuket and Langkawi in Malaysia. They post their offers on the notice boards and walls of restaurants. You have INSIDER TIP the best opportunities of contacting yachtsmen in the bay of Chalong and on Nai Harn Beach/Ao Sane. This is where most of the private sailing boats that come to Phuket put down anchor. Many leading boat charter companies are represented in the marinas on the east coast of Phuket, for example *Asia Marine Leisure (Boat Lagoon | www.asia-marine.net)*, or *Phuket Yachtcharter (Yacht Haven Marina | www.phuket-yachts.com)*.

SWIMMING & SNORKELLING

On Phuket as on all beaches in the south of Thailand, bear in mind that swimming can be dangerous in the rainy season between May and September. When red flags fly on the beaches, take them seriously. Every year tourists are carried out to sea by treacherous currents and drown. If you are swept away by a rip current, do not try to swim against it in panic (you will be completely exhausted after a couple of minutes), but try to swim out of it to the side. On Phuket snorkellers can still find corals close to the shore on *Kata Beach* and in the bay of *Ao Sane*. Better places for snorkelling are, for example, off *Ko He* (Coral Island) and *Ko Raya*, and of course all around *Ko Phi Phi* as well as around *Similan*, which is not only a top diving destination, the snorkelling is excellent too.

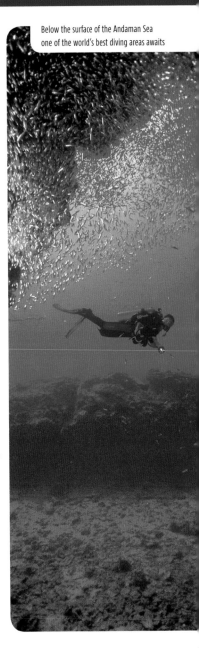
Below the surface of the Andaman Sea one of the world's best diving areas awaits

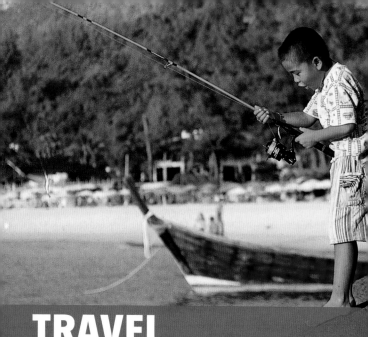

TRAVEL WITH KIDS

The chances of children finding friends to play with are higher on Phuket than anywhere else in Thailand, as many families come here for a holiday.

Phuket's beaches are one huge sandpit for children. However, some are more suitable than others. The central part of crowded Patong Beach is simply too crammed with loungers and sunshades. It is better to head for the less frequented northern and southern sections. Things are much quieter on the beaches of Bang Tao, Mai Khao, Nai Harn, Kata, Kata Noi and Karon. The bay of Ao Sane is not a suitable beach for children to swim, as corals and sharp-edged rocks can cause injury.

If your children get bored of beach life, you can take them for an elephant ride or play a round of mini-golf with dinosaurs. It is worth noting that Thailand is one of the world's leading producers of children's clothing, which is extremely cheap in comparison to Europe or North America.

THE WEST COAST

ADVENTURE MINIGOLF
(114 B3) *(𝒲 C7)*
Phuket's mini-golf course, with 18 holes, is near *Bang Tao Beach* on the main road in the north of the tourist village. Daily *11am–11pm | admission 280 baht, children 200 baht | tel. 08 72 68 19 25 | www. phuketadventureminigolf.com*

Photo: Kata Noi Beach

Dinosaurs and elephants, canoe tours and a climbing park – Phuket is holiday heaven for the whole family

DINO PARK, KARON BEACH ⭐
(116 A4) (*ØØ C11*)

Huge dinosaurs open their gaping, tooth-filled jaws, and after dark a fire-spitting volcano rumbles into action. All artificial, of course. This primeval land of fantasy is actually a crazy-golf course – fun for adults too! *Daily 10am–midnight | admission 240 baht, children 180 baht | Karon Rd. | on the hill between Kata and Karon Beach near the Marina Cottage resort | tel. 076 33 06 25 | www.dinopark. com*

ELEPHANT TREKS
(116 A2–4) (*ØØ C10–12*)

Elephants ceased to roam Phuket long ago, but tourism has brought them back. There are some 30 elephant camps on the island, especially in the south, for example along the road connecting Patong Beach and Karon Beach and the road from Kata Beach to the bay of Chalong.

Children love these animals, of course, and take great pleasure in a ride on the back of an elephant. The boom in elephant trekking on Phuket is not without its problems, as some owners are more interested in turning a quick baht than in looking after their animals. Some of them leave their elephants out in the blazing sun for too long, give them too little to eat or drink, and do not allow them enough breaks. Nevertheless, the *Elephant Help Foundation* regards tourism as advantageous on the whole, as it gives the *mahouts*, the owners and riders, an opportunity to earn money, which is ultimately in the best interests of the elephants themselves.

INSIDER TIP QUEST LAGUNA ADVENTURE (114 B2) (*m C7*)

An adventure playground with jungle terrain awaits visitors with a good head for heights at Bang Tao Beach. This place is often used by companies for training and bonding sessions, but in the *family fun zone* kids from the age of six can learn to climb or (with ropes) clamber around the treetops. A whole afternoon of fun for kids costs only 200 baht. *Laguna Beach Resort | Bang Tao Beach | tel. 076 31 42 53 | www.lagunaphuket.com/quest*

SPLASH JUNGLE, MAI KHAO BEACH (112 B2) (*m C2*)

There is no jungle at all in this aquapark, but the 'splashes' bit is true. The park's main attractions are a long flume, a pool with a wave machine and a water carousel *(Super Bowl)*. In the 335 m/365 yd-long 'Lazy River' adults and children can let the current carry them gently in rubber rings. *Daily 10am–6pm | admission 1295 baht, children 650 baht, under-fives free | West Sands Resort | Mai Khao Beach | tel. 076 37 21 11 | www.splashjunglewaterpark. com*

SOUTH AND EAST COAST

INSIDER TIP PHUKET RIDING CLUB, CHALONG (116 C4) (*m D12*)

Children too can get into the saddle here and trot through the rubber plantations or down to Mittrapab Beach. A guide accompanies the group. *Daily 7am–6.30pm | 1000 baht per hour | Viset Rd. | road to Rawai, approx. 1.5 km/1 mile south of the roundabout | Chalong | tel. 076 28 82 13 | www.phuket ridingclub. com*

SIAM SAFARI, CHALONG (116 C4) (*m D12*)

This tour operator, which has received various awards, offers a number of activities that children enjoy, such as Land Rover trips, canoe tours and elephant rides. At the Siam Safari headquarters you can see how skilful monkeys are at picking coconuts. *Headquarters daily 9am–5pm | 45 Chao Fa Rd. | bypass from the airport, north of the roundabout | Chalong | tel. 076 28 01 16 | www.siam safari.com*

SOI DOG FOUNDATION ☺ (112 B3) (*m D3*)

The dogs' home run by this organisation is financed entirely by donations. It looks after Phuket's strays and also welcomes visitors. North of the airport at Mai Khao Beach. For exact directions about how to get there, see the website. *Mon–Fri 8am–5pm | www.soidog.org*

PHUKET TOWN & AROUND

BUTTERFLY GARDEN & INSECTARIUM (117 D2) (*m E10*)

Over 40 kinds of butterflies flutter about in a tropical garden. The other insects are no less interesting. They include creatures that look like leaves or twigs. Visitors can walk inside an aviary with twittering tropical birds in all colours of the rainbow. In the *Silk Museum* you can learn all about silk worms and the production of shimmering fabric from their threads. *Daily 9am–5pm | admission 300 baht, children 150 baht, on the northern edge of town; coming from the town centre via Yaowaraj Rd., coming from Patong Beach via the road to the airport (signposted) | tel. 076 210861 | www.phuketbutterfly.com*

SIAM NIRAMIT ⭐ (115 D5) (*m E9*)

In a theatre seating 1750 that opened on Phuket in 2011, Niramit stages a gigantic show of culture and folklore *(Wed–Mon from 8.30pm)* that is equally fascinating for adults and children. A village including a floating market was built on the site, allowing you to gain an impression of rural life in the four regions of Thailand. The demonstrations include the production of silk and making children's toys from grass. You can also take your children for a couple of circuits on the back of the elephants that will perform in the show later. The Thai Village is open to visitors from 5.30pm. *Admission to show and village from 1500 baht, including buffet dinner from 1850 baht, children 1650 baht | pickup service by minibus from your hotel costs 300 baht per person (return) | northwest of Phuket Town on the bypass road to the airport, 3 km/2 miles north of the big Tesco Lotus supermarket | tel. 076 335000 | www.siam niramit.com*

Playing, running around, splashing and swimming: Phuket has lots of child-friendly beaches

FESTIVALS & EVENTS

Many religious festivals and tourist events have different dates each year. For an up-to-date calendar of events, refer to the tourist office and the websites named here. The local Phuket Gazette also publishes information about events and celebrations, and has listings in the online edition www.phuketgazette.net (click on Events Calendar).

PUBLIC HOLIDAYS

1 Jan *New Year's Day;* **Full moon in February** *Makha Pucha,* commemoration of Buddha's sermon to 1250 believers; **6 April** *Chakri Day,* foundation of the Chakri dynasty in 1782; **13–15 April** *Songkran,* Thai New Year celebrations; **1 May** *Day of Labour;* **5 May** *Coronation Day, of King* Bhumibol Adulyadej (Rama IX); **Full moon in May** *Visakha Pucha,* commemoration of Buddha's birth, enlightenment and death; **Full moon in July** *Asaha Pucha,* commemoration of Buddha's first sermon. One day later, *Khaopansa* is the start of the Buddhist fasting period; **12 Aug** *Birthday of Queen Sirikit,* the wife of Rama IX); **23 Oct** *Chulalongkorn Day,* day of the death of King Chulalongkorn); **5 Dec** *Birthday of King Bhumibol;* **10 Dec** *Constitution Day;* 31 Dec *New Year's Eve*

FESTIVALS & EVENTS

JANUARY/FEBRUARY

▶ *Phuket Old Town Festival:* Fair in the old quarter. Music and shows take spectators back in the history of the island capital, which was greatly influenced by the Chinese ▶ INSIDER TIP *Chinese New Year:* week-long *temple festival* at Wat Chalong on the bypass, road no. 4022, between Phuket Town and Rawai Beach. Fair, beauty contest, fireworks

FEBRUARY/MARCH

▶ *Gay Pride Festival:* Parade on Patong Beach. For the exact date see *www.phuket-pride.org*

APRIL

▶ *Songkran:* No other Thai festival is celebrated as joyously as New Year. Battles on the water are held. At the beach of Nai Yang, sea turtles are released from the Laem Phan Wa breeding station.
▶ *Phuket Bike Week:* Motorbike fans tour the island. Parties and events on Patong Beach. For the dates, see *www.phuketbikeweek.com*

Red-hot coals, a romantic full moon and water battles – festivals on Phuket combine religion and love of life

MAY/JUNE & OCTOBER/NOVEMBER

▶ INSIDER TIP *Loi Rüa:* Festival of the *Chao Leh* (sea gypsies) on Rawai Beach at the beginning and end of the monsoon season. Bamboo rafts supposedly carry all misfortune – in the shape of replica weapons and cut-off hair – out to sea.

AUGUST/SEPTEMBER

▶ *Phuket Marathon:* Also a half- marathon, walking (5km/3 miles) and children's run (2km/1.25 miles). *www.phuketmarathon.com*

SEPTEMBER/OCTOBER

▶ ★ ● *Vegetarian Festival:* In honour of nine divine kings, who according to a legend ruled in China for 45,600 years. Chinese Thais eat vegetarian food for nine days, enter a trance and flagellate themselves in processions through Phuket Town: they walk over red-hot coas and stick spikes and hooks through their cheeks and tongue. Visitors should wear white clothing. *www.phuketvegetarian.com*

NOVEMBER

▶ *Loi Kratong:* The most romantic festival in Thailand. At full moon, boats are placed in the water with a candle, joss sticks, coins and flowers – on rivers, lakes and canals, on Phuket on swimming pools too. The water goddess *Mae Khongka* is asked for forgiveness for polluting the water.

DECEMBER

▶ *King's Cup Regatta:* Yachts from all over the world compete by sailing off the southern tip of Phuket in early December. *www.kingscup.com*
▶ *Patong Carnival:* Shows, live concerts, fireworks and a parade – celebrations for the start of the high season for tourism lasting several days.

LINKS, BLOGS, APPS & MORE

LINKS

▶ www.phuket.com Hotels, restaurants, nightlife, shopping, tours, beaches ... more or less every subject that could interest visitors to the island can be found here

▶ www.phuketemagazine.com For beaches and restaurants, lifestyle and shopping – this online magazine operated by the Phuket tourist office presents the island, and has a lot of beautiful photos

▶ http://www.phuket.net/ Useful tips not only for holidaymakers, but for those planning to stay longer thanks to a section on ‚living on Phuket'

▶ www.phuketbestevent.com To find out what is going on, take a look at this site. It also provides lots of information about eating and drinking, art and culture, and other subjects that are of interest to tourists

▶ http://www.faqs.org/faqs/thai/culture/ The history and culture of Thailand, Buddhism, Thai cuisine – not a colourful or hip website, but lots of solid information about the country and its people

▶ www.travelfish.org Specialised in low-budget accommodation. This site states plainly what is good and bad, and is the coolest address on the web if you are looking for low-cost accommodation

BLOGS

▶ www.jamie-monk.blogspot.com Jamie explores the island, getting off the beaten track, and presents almost everything that you can see and do on Phuket in his blog

▶ www.phuket101.net Where can I get grilled insects? Where are the finest historic townhouses – and the wildest parties? The answers to these and other questions, as well as cool photos, can be found on this site

▶ www.timinphuket.blogspot.de Tim takes you along with him to the mar-

Regardless of whether you are still preparing your trip or already in Phuket: these addresses will provide you with more information, videos and networks to make your holiday even more enjoyable.

kets and the beach, to restaurants, temples and everywhere else he goes on Phuket

▶ www.phuketdining.com/ This is not just a website about eating out on Phuket. It also has information on many other subjects, and a collection of videos about diving, cookery courses, restaurants, nightlife and many other themes

▶ www.vimeo.com This huge collection of videos from Phuket includes hints for enjoying the scenery, dining, shopping and sightseeing, as well as a good deal about the seamier side of tourist life on the island

▶ www.phuketbesttv.com Fashion shows, parties and rock concerts – whenever there is something happening, Phuket Best TV is there to film it

▶ www.phuketgazette.net/tv Phuket's main English-language newspaper uploads videos

▶ Phuket Map and Walking Tours This iPhone app will not only show you the way to the sights of Phuket Town, but can also be your guide to the nightlife on Patong Beach

▶ Phuketcity An app for iPhone and Android, specialised in hotel bookings

▶ Phuket Island – GPS Map Navigator Wherever you may be on Phuket – the navigator on your iPhone willl find you and give you directions

▶ Amazing Thailand Phuket Even when you are offline, the state tourist office will provide information on your iPhone

▶ http://www.expat-blog.com/ Lots of Westerners live on Phuket permanently or for much of the year. Some of them share their experiences on this site.

▶ www.hospitalityclub.org and www.couchsurfing.org These worldwide hospitality networks have members on Phuket who provide free accommodation for their visitors

TRAVEL TIPS

ACCOMMODATION

In the peak season from about 15 December to 10 January, many resorts charge supplements of 10 to 20 per cent. In the off-peak season (April to October) price reductions of up to 40 per cent are possible. You can sometimes save a lot of money by booking via internet, directly or through a hotel reservation service such as *www.phuket-hotels.com* and *www.asiarooms.com*. For last-minute bargains, try *www.latestays.com*. Booking a package holiday can be cheaper than making your own arrangements. At many resorts guests must pay a steep price for compulsory dinner at Christmas and New Year. Check this in advance if you book a hotel at this time of the year. For details of hotels and their location, see *www.2phuket.com*. For reviews by guests, refer to *www.tripadvisor.com*.

RESPONSIBLE TRAVEL

It doesn't take a lot to be environmentally friendly whilst travelling. Don't just think about your carbon footprint whilst flying to and from your holiday destination but also about how you can protect nature and culture abroad. As a tourist it is especially important to respect nature, look out for local products, cycle instead of driving, save water and much more. If you would like to find out more about eco-tourism please visit: *www.ecotourism.org*

ARRIVAL

any operators of charter flights *(see www.phuketairportonline.com)* go to Phuket directly from Europe. You'll find cheap flights at *www.flightcentre.co.uk; www.cheapticket.co.uk; www.cheapflights. co.uk; www.travelsupermarket.com; www. southalltravel.co.uk* and many other internet agencies, but it's also worth contacting airlines such as Qatar Airways direct. Bangkok's new international Suvarnabhumi airport (pronounced: *Suwannapum | www.airportsuvarnabhumi.com)* is a hub for Southeast Asia and served by most European and Asian airlines. Flight time from London is approx. 11 hours. Even during the December/January high season, non-stop return flights from London to Bangkok with major airlines such British Airways or Thai Airways are available for around £900 (US-$ 1400); cheap return flights to Bangkok or Phuket with one stopover can be had for as little as £400 (US-$ 630). From Suvarnabhumi, Thai Airways and Bangkok Airways *(www. bangkokair.com)* fly to Phuket several times daily. Prices vary greatly according to the time of day and season. You can normally expect to pay between 50 and 80 euros one way. Since October 2012 budget airline Air Asia *(www.airasia.com)* has flown to Phuket only from the old airport, Don Muang. A further budget airline, Nok Air *(www.nokair.com)*, operates a service from Dong Muang. The flight from there to Phuket costs approx. 1,300 baht. From the airport in Phuket, the bus to the terminal in Phuket Town costs 90 baht. The limousine service will take you to all beaches for a fixed amount but costs twice as much as a public taxi. To find the taxi rank, go right when you leave the arrivals concourse. Before setting off make sure that the driver is willing to switch on the meter – they do not always want to do so, especially during rush hour.

BANKS & CREDIT CARDS

At banks you can change travellers' cheques denominated in dollars and other currencies *(Mon–Fri 8.30am–3.30pm, bureaux de change daily, often until 10pm)*. If you pay by credit card, many shops increase the price. You can also get cash with your credit card by showing a passport, but this is usually easier at a cashpoint (ATM). Visa and MasterCard are accepted by all banks. At many cashpoints bearing the Maestro sign you can get cash using your normal bank card. Branches of Bangkok Bank also accept American Express. A fee of 150 baht is charged per cash withdrawal. If you lose your card, do not fail to inform your bank immediately.

CAR HIRE

A rental car is a good way of exploring the island (Jeeps for about approx. 1000 baht, air-conditioned cars approx. 1600 baht per day, reductions for longer hire periods). Hire desks for Avis *(tel. 076 35 12 43 | www.avisthailand.com)* and Budget *(tel. 076 20 53 96 | www.budget.co.th)* are situated at the airport and in large hotels. *Pure Car Rent (Phuket Town | 75 Rasada Rd. | tel. 076 21 10 02 | www.purecarrent.com)* has a good reputation. Traffic drives on the left. An international driving licence is required. Ensure you

BUDGETING	
Beer	1.45 £/ 2.20 $
	for 0.3 litres in a bar
Beach	4.50 £/6.50 $
lounger	*for two and a sunshade per day*
Massage	7 £/10 $
	on the beach
Soup	0.80 £/1.20 $
	for noodle soup at a food stall
Petrol	0.80 £/1.20 $
	for a litre
Pineapple	0.20 £/ 0.30 $
	for a whole fruit

have insurance that includes damage to persons as well as to property. Reputable agencies have the appropriate policies. Avoid car-hire agencies at the roadside which offer private cars or other vehicles which are not registered as hire cars. What might look like a bargain could turn out to be very expensive. A hire-car with driver is worth considering as an alternative to driving yourself *(adding approx. 500 baht to the cost, for 8 hours)*.

CHILD PROTECTION

At night children go from bar to bar, selling cigarettes, chewing gum and flowers, especially on Patong Beach. The child protection organisation *Childwatch Phuket (www.childwatchphuket.org)* states: 'The more they sell, the more certain it is that they will have to work into the early hours. However appealing their eyes, and however much sympathy you feel for them, it is better for the children if you buy nothing.'

CLIMATE, WHEN TO GO

In the period from November to February the weather is what many Europeans and North Americans regard as an ideal summer. After that, and until May, it gets very hot and does not cool off much at night. In the rainy season (May to October/November) temperatures fall a little. Most rain falls between mid-August and mid-October.

CONSULATES & EMBASSIES

UK EMBASSY
14 Wireless Road | Lumpini, Pathumwan | Bangkok 10330 | tel. 0 23 05 83 33 | www.ukinthailand.fco.gov.uk | Mon–Thu 8am–noon and 12:45pm–4:30pm; Fri 8am–1pm

US EMBASSY
American Citizen Services | U.S. Embassy | 95 Wireless Road | Bangkok 10330 | tel. 0 22 05 40 49 | www.bangkok.usembassy.gov | Mon–Fri 7:30–11am and 1–2pm

UK HONORARY CONSULATE
If you require consular assistance in Phuket, please call the British Embassy in Bangkok on 02 305 8333 and follow the instructions to speak to a member of consular staff.

CUSTOMS

Cash amounting to more than 10,000 US dollars must be declared on arrival in Thailand. It is forbidden to export statues of Buddha. Export of antiques and animal products requires a permit. Travellers returning to the European Union have the following duty-free allowance: 200 cigarettes, 250 g of tobacco or 50 cigars, 2 litres of wine and 1 litre of spirits, 500 g of coffee, 50 g of perfume, 250 ml of eau de toilette and other goods to a value of £ 390/560 US dollars (when flying). When entering the USA, goods to a value of $ 800 including 2 litres of alcoholic drinks are duty-free (see *www.cbp.gov* for all details).

ELECTRICITY

220-volt power supply. Adapters are sold in electric goods shops.

HEALTH

No vaccinations are necessary. It is not advisable to drink tap water. However, you need not have reservations about eating street food, even from basic stalls, as Thais are careful about preparing snacks and meals. Medical care on Phuket is excellent. The best hospital on the island is the *Bangkok Phuket Hospital (tel. 076 25 44 21 | www.phukethospital.com)*, and the *Phuket International Hospital (tel. 076 25 44 21 | www.phuket-inter-hospital.co.th)* also meets international standards. English-speaking staff are present at both. Contact the hospitals to get an ambulance. The dentists on the island also have high standards at prices much lower than in Europe and the USA.

IMMIGRATION

For a visit not exceeding 30 days, visitors from many countries, including the UK, do not need a visa to enter Thailand, just a passport valid for at least 6 months, and a return or onward ticket. Visas can usually be extended by up to 10 days at immigration offices throughout the country. If you plan to stay more than a month, obtain a 60-day visa at a Thai consulate or embassy in your country before leaving home. Check *www.thaivisa.com* or the websites of Thailand's immigration authority (*www.im*

migration.go.th) and the Ministry of Foreign Affairs *(www.mfa.go.th)* for details.

DIPLOMATIC REPRESENTATION

UK: *Royal Thai Embassy in London | 29–30 Queen's Gate | London SW7 5JB | tel. 030 79 48 10 | www.thaiembassyuk.org.uk*
US: *Royal Thai Embassy in Washington | 1024 Wisconsin Ave. | N.W. Washington D.C. 20007 | tel. 202 9 44 36 00 | www.thaiembdc.org*

INFORMATION

THAILAND TOURIST AUTHORITY (TAT)
UK: *17–19 Cockspur Street | London SW1Y 5BL | tel. 0870 900 2007 | www.tourismthailand.org*
US: *Broadway, Suite 2810 | New York, NY 10006 | tel. 212/432-0433 | www.tourismthailand.org*
Australia: *Level 20, 56 Pit Street | Sydney, NSW 2000 | tel. (02) 9247 7549 | www.tourismthailand.org*

TOURISM AUTHORITY OF THAILAND (TAT)
Information desk at the airport. *191 Thalang Rd. | tel. 076 211036, tel. 076 212213 |*

INTERNET

Information about Phuket can be found on many websites: *www.phuketdelight.com*, *www.phuket.com*, *www.phukettourism.org* and *www.phuket-online.com*. Beaches are listed at *www.phuket.as*. The best weather website is *www.phuketweather.blogspot.com*. See *www.phuketmaps.com* for maps of the beaches.

INTERNET CAFÉS & WIFI

Internet cafés can be found all over Phuket. They charge approx. 1 baht per minute. The i-net PCs in hotel lobbies are usually much more expensive. Many resorts, restaurants and cafés have Wi-Fi. Although restaurants usually provide the service for free, many resorts charge up to 200 baht per hour. If you want to surf with your own device, ask in advance how much your resort charges per hour or day. You only pay a few baht per minute to surf using a modem and a Thai internet SIM card. The cards are available in many shops and in the minimarkets of the 7-Eleven chain.

PHONE & MOBILE PHONE

The country code for the UK is 0044, for the USA and Canada 001, for Ireland

CURRENCY CONVERTER

£	THB	THB	£
1	48.75	10	0.21
3	146	30	0.62
5	244	50	1.03
13	634	130	2.67
40	1,950	400	8.21
75	3,656	750	15.38
120	5,850	1,200	24.61
250	12,188	2,500	51.28
500	24,376	5,000	102.56

$	THB	THB	$
1	30	10	0.33
3	90	30	1
5	150	50	1.67
13	390	130	4.34
40	1,200	400	13.34
75	2,249	750	25
120	3,598	1,200	40
250	7,495	2,500	83.40
500	14,990	5,000	166.78

For current exchange rates see www.xe.com

00353. Then dial the town or area code without a zero. The code for phoning Phuket from abroad is 006676. Phone cards for public telephones are available from post/telecommunications offices and many shops. The better hotels have IDD phones in the rooms, enabling guests to make international calls direct, usually at high rates. Phoning with your mobile phone usually incurs roaming charges, and you bear part of the costs of incoming calls. To avoid this, you can replace your SIM card from home with a Thai SIM card. Pre-paid cards are on sale everywhere. Thai providers of mobile telephony often offer particular country codes at special rates. True Move, for example, offers calls to Europe via internet from 1 baht per minute. On average a call to Europe using a special code costs 8 baht. The three main providers are AIS *(www.ais.co.th/12call/en/index.html)*, DTAC *(www.happy.co.th/home_en.php)* and True Move *(www.truemove.com/en/Inter-SIM-Prepay.rails)*. In many shops you can get a low-price second mobile phone for using a Thai SIM card. Basic mobile phones are sold for approx. 20 euros, second-hand ones for even less.

WEATHER IN PHUKET

	Jan	Feb	March	April	May	June	July	Aug	Sept	Oct	Nov	Dec
Daytime temperatures in °C/°F												
	31/88	32/90	33/91	33/91	31/88	31/88	30/86	30/86	30/86	30/86	30/86	31/88
Nighttime temperatures in °C/°F												
	22/72	22/72	23/73	24/75	24/75	25/77	24/75	25/77	24/75	24/75	23/73	22/72
Sunshine hours/day												
	9	9	8	8	7	6	6	6	6	5	5	7
Precipitation days/month												
	4	4	7	15	20	19	17	18	20	20	15	8
Water temperature in °C/°F												
	27/81	28/82	29/84	29/84	29/84	29/84	28/82	28/82	28/82	28/82	28/82	27/81

POST

Airmail to Europe and North America up to 10 g costs 17 baht, postcards 15 baht. It normally takes 5 to 7 days for letters and cards to arrive. Air-mail parcels (5 kg) cost about 2500 baht. The main post office is in Phuket Town *(Montri Rd. | Mon–Fri 8.30am–4.30pm, Sat 9am–12 noon).*

PRICES & CURRENCY

The main unit of Thai currency, the *baht*, is divided into 100 *satang*. Notes of 20, 50, 100, 500 and 1000 baht are in circulation. The small coins of 25 and 50 satang are given as change in supermarkets and almost nowhere else. Coins for 1, 2, 5 and 10 baht are more usual. A meal with rice at a basic eatery costs no more than 60 baht. A two-course menu seldom costs more than 250 baht. Prices are fixed in supermarkets and big shopping centres. Elsewhere you bargain. Thais do not regard it as unfair to charge foreigners more. A two-price system is perfectly usual in many privately run establishments such as zoos and fun parks. State institutions such as national parks and museums also have higher admission prices for foreigners.

PUBLIC TRANSPORT

There is one major drawback to public transport: buses and covered pick-ups with bench seating are cheap, but they only run between 7am and approx. 5pm – and then only from the beaches to Phuket Town *(to Ranong Rd., near the roundabout)*. If you want to go from one beach to another without a detour via the town, or to travel in the evening, you have to hire a tuk tuk – and bargain! Taxis with a meter are only based at the airport.

TOURIST POLICE

Nationwide emergency hotline: *tel. 1155.* Station in Phuket Town: *100/31-32, Chalermphakeat Rd. (Bypass Rd. towards the airport, opposite Gems Gallery) | phuketdir.com/pkttouristpolice*

TRANSCRIPTION

There is no generally applicable system of transcribing Thai words and names in the Roman alphabet, which means you see various spellings of some words.

TIME

Thailand time is GMT plus 7 hours throughout the year (New York plus 14 hours, Australia minus 3 hours).

TIPPING

In many better restaurants there is a service charge of ten per cent. You should then pay a tip only if the service was especially good. Ten per cent is a suitable tip in restaurants without a service charge. Taxi drivers do not normally get a tip.

NOTES

FOR YOUR NEXT HOLIDAY ...

MARCO POLO TRAVEL GUIDES

- PACKED WITH INSIDER TIPS
- BEST WALKS AND TOURS
- FULL-COLOUR PULL-OUT MAP
  AND STREET ATLAS

ROAD ATLAS

The green line ▬ indicates the Trips & Tours (p. 84–89)
The blue line ▬ indicates The perfect route (p. 30–31)

All tours are also marked on the pull-out map

Photo: Karon Beach

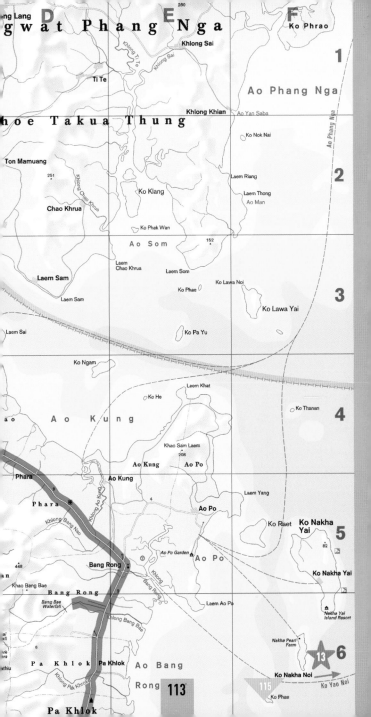

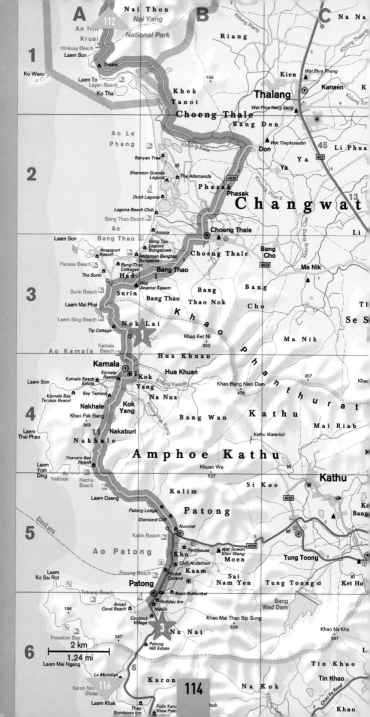

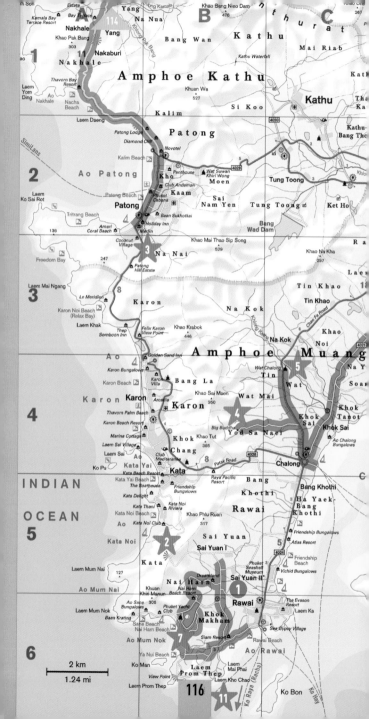

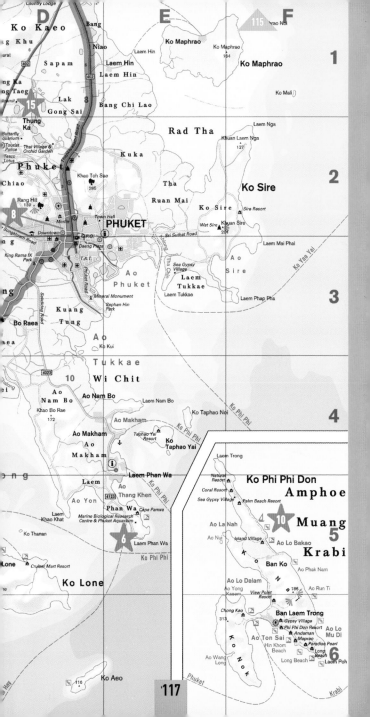

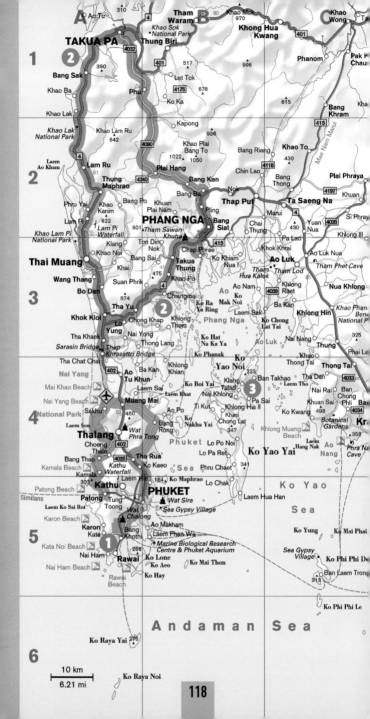

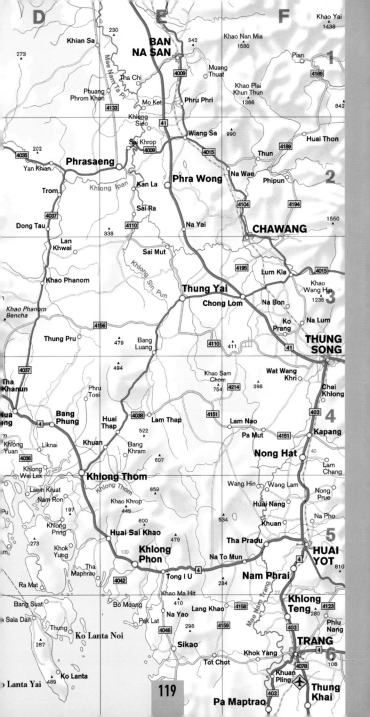

KEY TO ROAD ATLAS

Highway Fernverkehrsstraße Grande route de transit Strada di transito	Hospital Krankenhaus Hôpital Ospedale
Main road Hauptstraße Route principale Strada principale	Police Polizei Police Polizia
Secondary road Nebenstraße Route secondaire Strada secondaria	Broadcasting station Funkstation Station radio Stazione radio
Carriage way, Path Fahrweg, Pfad Chemin carrosable, Sentier Strada carrozzabile, Sentiero	Waterfall Wasserfall Cascade Cascata
Petrol station Tankstelle Station essence Stazione di rifornimento	Golf Golf Golf Golf
Distance in km Entfernung in km Distance en km Distanze in km	Harbour Hafen Port Porto
County boundary Bezirksgrenze Frontière de province Confine di provincia	Point of interest Sehenswürdigkeit Curiosité Curiosità
Parish boundary Gemeindegrenze Front. de commune Conf. di municipio	Hotel Hotel Hôtel Albergo
Airport Flughafen Aéroport Aeroporto	Beach Strand Plage Spiaggia
Information Information Informations Informazione	Scuba diving Sporttauchen Sous-marine plongée Sport subaqueo
Buddhist temple Buddha-Tempel Temple bouddhique Tempio buddista	Waterskiing Wasserski Ski nautique Sci nautico
Chinese temple Chinesischer Tempel Temple chinois Tempio cinese	Yachting Segelsport Centre de voile Sport velico
Mosque Moschee Mosquée Moschea	View point Aussichtspunkt Vue panoramique Panorama
Church Kirche Église Chiesa	National park Nationalpark Parc national Parco nazionale
Monument Denkmal Monument Monumento	Trips & Tours Ausflüge & Touren Excursions & tours Gite & escursione
Post office Postamt Poste Posta	Perfect route Perfekte Route
MARCO POLO Highlight	

INDEX

This index lists all sights, islands (Ko), beaches and bays, destinations for trips and important persons or themes mentioned in the guide. Page numbers in bold refer to the main entry.

CREDITS

WRITE TO US

e-mail: info@marcopologuides.co.uk

Did you have a great holiday?
Is there something on your mind?
Whatever it is, let us know!
Whether you want to praise, alert us
to errors or give us a personal tip –
MARCO POLO would be pleased to
hear from you.
We do everything we can to provide the
very latest information for your trip.

Nevertheless, despite all of our authors'
thorough research, errors can creep in.
MARCO POLO does not accept any
liability for this. Please contact us by
e-mail or post.

MARCO POLO Travel Publishing Ltd
Pinewood, Chineham Business Park
Crockford Lane, Chineham
Basingstoke, Hampshire RG24 8AL
United Kingdom

PICTURE CREDITS
Cover Photograph: Long Tail Boat, picture-alliance: Robert Harding World Imagery (Emmerson)
Images: Brush Restaurant (17 bottom); DuMont Bildarchiv: Sasse (78, 101, 110/111); W. Hahn (1 bottom, 6, 36, 53, 60); Huber: Schmid (flap r., 10/11, 30 l., 120/121), Stadler (26 r.); ©iStockphoto.com: Paul Pegler (16 centre), ShyMan (16 top); M. Kirchgessner (28); Laif: Amme (30 r., 38), Heuer (9, 45), Sasse (flap l., 3 top, 3 bottom, 34, 40, 54, 66/67, 84/85); Mai Khao Marine Turtle Foundation: Ornjaree Nawee (16 bottom); mauritius images: Alamy (8, 18/19, 64, 68, 87, 88), ib (Kreder) (4), ib (Stadler) (2 o., 5, 81, 82), ib (Stella) (97); H. Mielke (3 centre, 12/13, 29, 74/75, 90/91, 93); picture-alliance: Robert Harding World Imagery (Emmerson) (1 top); O. Stadler (2 centre bottom, 2 bottom, 24/25, 32/33, 57, 58/59, 76/77, 94/95); O. Stadler & A. Stubhan (15, 20, 21, 22, 26 l., 27, 47, 49, 71, 72, 98 l., 100 top, 100 bottom); T. Stankiewicz (42, 50, 63); Tree Pony (17 top); M. Weigt (2 centre top, 7, 28/29, 98/99)

1st Edition 2014
Worldwide Distribution: Marco Polo Travel Publishing Ltd, Pinewood, Chineham Business Park, Crockford Lane, Basingstoke, Hampshire RG24 8AL, United Kingdom. Email: sales@marcopolouk.com
© MAIRDUMONT GmbH & Co. KG, Ostfildern
Chief editor: Marion Zorn
Author: Wilfried Hahn, Editor: Cordula Natusch
Programme supervision: Anita Dahlinger, Ann-Katrin Kutzner, Nikolai Michaelis
Picture editor: Gabriele Forst
What's hot: wunder media, Munich
Cartography road atlas: © Berndtson & Berndtson Productions GmbH, Fürstenfeldbruck;
Cartography pull-out map: © Berndtson & Berndtson Productions GmbH, Fürstenfeldbruck
Design: milchhof:atelier, Berlin; Front cover, pull-out map cover, page 1: factor product münchen
Translated from German by John Sykes, Cologne; editor of the English edition: Kathleen Becker, Lisbon
Prepress: BW-Medien GmbH, Leonberg

DOS & DON'TS ☞

Here are a few hints for a carefree holiday

UNDERESTIMATING THE SUN

A lot of tourists sit on deck on the ferries to the islands. The wind cools their faces, they don't notice that the sun is shining as intensely as on the beach – and arrive with severe sunburn. Use sun-blocker, and better still shield your skin from the sun altogether on ferries. Think hat!

DRIVING A MOTORBIKE WITHOUT A HELMET

Motorcyclists and their passengers are obliged to wear helmets. You can often see three or four locals on a motorbike without helmets, but tourists should not emulate them, as it is no use pointing out what the locals do if you are stopped at one of the frequent police checks. On average there is one fatal accident every day, and tourists are regularly among the casualties. Note also that the only third-party insurance available for using a motorbike covers injuries to others only up to a sum of 15,000 baht.

RUNNING AWAY FROM DOGS

Stray dogs are a common sight on Phuket. During the day they are harmless, but at night and when they roam in a pack, they can be a real nuisance. On no account run away. Walk at a steady pace without hurrying. One trick that almost always works is to bend down as if about to pick up a stone. Then the dogs will keep their distance.

GETTING CARRIED AWAY WITH A WATER SCOOTER

You can zip over the waves on a water scooter, but it might be an annoyance to others and even cause serious injuries. On Phuket they are only allowed on the beaches of Bang Tao, Karon, Kata and Patong. If you zoom off to another beach, you can be fined.

FEELING TOO SECURE

Southern Thailand is a safe place to travel on the whole, but do pay attention to a few guidelines about staying safe. Women should not walk on lonely beaches or hitchhike unaccompanied. Be on your guard in the tourist areas of Phuket on little-used roads at night – foreigners riding mopeds have been attacked and robbed. Flashing a well-filled wallet around in a bar can arouse desires. If invited to join locals for a drinking session, say no politely or leave after having one drink, as pent-up frustrations can be explosive when Thais get drunk.

IGNORING RED FLAGS

From early May until November or December dangerous rip currents often occur on Phuket's beaches. There are fatalities every year because holidaymakers ignore the red flags and enter the water.